# THE SKETCHER

Julie Riedel

The Sketcher

Copyright ©2022 Julie Riedel


ISBN    979-8-218-00600-6    Print
ISBN    979-8-218-00601-3    eBook


Library of Congress Control Number 2022909023





Disclaimer:

I have tried to recreate events, locales and conversations from my memories of them. In order to maintain their anonymity, in some instances I have changed the names of individuals and places, and I may have changed some identifying characteristics and details such as physical properties, occupations and places of residence.


Book design by Nan Barnes, StoriesToTellBooks.com

*Thanks to S.G. Conner*

*for her assistance in writing this book.*

# Contents

# Dedication

*To my children,*

*John, Jessica, Jackie, James and Rudy*

*and to the victims' families.*

# Preface

Julie Riedel is "The Sketcher." She was the first artist in the history of criminology to age a serial killer in drawings. As a college senior doing an independent study in Forensic Drawing, an investigator with the Wichita Police Department in Wichita, Kansas, gave her access to the BTK serial killer's 10 cold case files. BTK's identity was unknown at the time. He was known only by his self-assigned initials BTK (Bind them, Torture them, and Kill them). In the summer of 1991, the case was stalled. It had been over 17 years since his first murders. Julie's assignment was to age the flip-chart-produced, 26-year-old face of this monster to age 46 or 47. At Julie's hands, BTK's middle-aged face came alive in a series of drawings showing the stress in his age-lined face. First with a full head of hair, then with male-patterned baldness, then with a moustache, and finally, clean shaven.

Julie's sketches of BTK were broadcast on television stations across the country and discussed in meetings among police, the Kansas Bureau of Investigation (KBI), and FBI investigators. To protect her and her family, Julie's name was never used in conjunction with her drawings of BTK, but his horrific crimes fueled her nightmares for 13 years and led her to fear for her children's safety. She saw danger everywhere.

In this book, the author assiduously avoids framing serial killer Dennis Rader's personality or his motives, except to describe how his evil affected others. He is a narcissist. Speaking of him from other than a cold, factual perspective was intentional for the purpose of not feeding his ego in any way. He is a footnote compared to the suffering of his victims.

*The Sketcher* tells the story of Julie Riedel's life and accomplishments, paralleled with her involvement in the BTK case. She wants her experiences to demonstrate that it is possible to find confidence and happiness after the neglect and mistreatment she suffered in childhood, to survive unhappy marriages fueled by anger, alcohol and drugs, and to break the cycles of violence, as she did when she raised her own children. She gave her kids the encouragement, respect, and love that was denied her and her seven brothers. Inspired by her five children, Julie shows how strength of will motivated her to overcome the damage from abusive relationships. In pushing beyond her feelings of inadequacies and fear, she succeeded professionally in her first love—art—and personally with her other first loves, her children.

*There are two great days in a person's life—
the day we are born and the day we discover why.*

~William Barclay

## Chapter 1

# Beginning of the End

*It's him!*

My heart slammed against my chest, forcing the air from my lungs. The dark moment stretched into oblivion. A smile contorted his face. A plastic bag in his hand. Death in his eyes held me in a grim embrace.

*Oh, God, I can't move. I need to save my babies.*

Wordless, he moved the bag over my head and wrapped it tightly around my neck. It was the last thing I remembered before I jerked awake, my chest heaving in search of air that my nightmare denied me. A cold sweat chilled me.

It was *the* dream, the one that repeated night after night until it became a part of me.

Still awake, my alarm shocked the silence at 5 a.m. This was the day I would deliver the final sketches of his face as it had aged in 20 years. Now that I had created his image on paper, his previously blank face now had features in my nightmares.

---

A few short months before, I was a 30-year-old single mother with two beautiful children. Separated from my alcoholic, unemployed husband, I struggled financially. As a young woman aching to succeed at what I did best—sketching and graphic design—I was in my final year of study at Wichita State University. It should have been easy. My mother told me I was born with a pencil in my hand, but the path was littered with the emotional fragments of a life that left me feeling small, isolated, and unworthy.

By late spring of 1992, I had transfigured my talent into a

vaguely defined dream. I was devoted to translating moments and emotion into visions on paper, inspired by the Life Drawing courses, where I learned the basic forms of the human body. Concentrating on the skeletal structures, musculature, and Leonardo Da Vinci's studies, I discovered an interest in forensic drawing and chose it for my final credits to graduate.

The curriculum didn't offer a class in forensic drawing. My advisor suggested an independent study course. I applied for and received permission. Professor Terry May was my mentor for the course. His encouragement during that time kept me going when my insecurities pushed me to retreat.

Professor May met with me in his small office in the Duerksen Fine Arts Center. I knocked softly and opened the door to a comfortably messy room with books stacked randomly on shelves. An ancient oak chair faced a battered wooden desk, behind which Professor May stood, smiling. "Hi, Julie, it's good to see you again."

"Good to see you again too, Professor."

He gestured to the chair. "I understand you want to do an independent study in forensic drawing. You were an excellent student in all the other classes you took from me. I'm confident you're going to do well in this one, too."

I sat, holding my arms tightly across my chest, shoulders up, trying to disappear into my own body. "Thank you, sir."

"Please, call me Terry."

"Okay, sir ... uh ... Terry. How should I start?" A deep breath restored me.

*Why am I so nervous? I know Professor May.*

Old feelings of inadequacy were habits I learned early in life and were hard to break.

"The Wichita Police Department is a good place to begin."

"So, uh, what do I say?" I envisioned the police laughing me back into my shell. I was inexperienced dealing with people in authority like the police.

"Explain that you're using an independent study in forensic drawing for college credit and ask if they'll help you. They'll probably give you an old crime file to work on. Your drawings of the suspect will be your final grade."

"Okay." I hedged. "I'll try."

I was scared shitless … quaking in my well-worn boots at the prospect of walking into the Wichita Police Department. So few people had believed in me during my life, and I doubted professional criminologists would take me seriously.

Professor May sensed my hesitancy. "You're fully capable of doing this, Julie. You're a gifted artist. Apply what you know and research the rest."

As I drove down Central toward Main, the Bartlett pear trees were blooming white and crisp on this unseasonably cold, late spring day … one I would rather be spending at home, sketching my children as they played. But I was driving to the detectives' squad at Wichita City Hall.

*You can do this, Julie, you are a gifted artist.*

It was my new mantra. It propelled me toward whatever fate awaited me.

The first view of my destination intimidated me. Everything that could go wrong replayed in my mind. Wichita City Hall was imposing in a late-19th century, governmental sort of way.

My appointment was on the second floor. I took the stairs, postponing the meeting as long as possible.

*You can do this, Julie, you are a gifted artist.*

Taking a deep breath and squaring my shoulders, I introduced myself to the receptionist. "I'm Julie Riedel, and I have an appointment with Officer Ken Landwehr."

"Have a seat over there. I'll let him know you're here."

The "seat over there" was a hard bench occupied by two people who looked like felons. I felt my confidence slipping toward the edge of an abyss.

*Will Officer Landwehr mistake me for one of the lawless-looking inhabitants of the bench and keep walking?*

"Miss Riedel?" The officer was tall and handsome with the serious demeanor of a man who had seen more distressing things in his life than this frightened slip of a woman could imagine. "What can I do for you?"

"Hi." We shook hands. "I'm studying art at WSU and have permission to do an independent study in forensic drawing. Professor May said you might be able to help me." I handed him the letter Professor May has provided to introduce me. He had written that I was a student with a high grade-point average and several awards for my artwork under my belt. I saw unspoken opportunity in the officer's eyes as he read the letter.

"Sure, stay here, I'll be right back."

I fidgeted beside my benchmates for the next 15 minutes before Officer Landwehr returned with a two-wheeled dolly stacked high with cardboard file boxes.

He led me into a small, stale-smelling room populated by a lacerated metal table and two well-worn chairs. Opening a file, he began, "These boxes contain the cold case files for the BTK strangler. I'd like you to draw sketches of what he looked like as he aged from around twenty-six to about forty-six or forty-seven. To my knowledge, this hasn't been done before. You'll be breaking new ground."

I was speechless. The crimes committed by BTK were the stuff of nightmares in the Wichita metropolitan area. His reign of terror lasted from January 1974 through January 1991, when he strangled his 10th victim. At that point he stopped killing and began taunted the press and police, taking credit for his past crimes and threatening more horror. No one knew who he was. Suspicion reigned in and around the city. He could have been your next-door neighbor, your electrician, telephone repairman, or the guy staring at you in the grocery store. He could have been your own husband or brother.

I stared at Officer Landwehr. This distinguished, no-nonsense man had just asked me to do a job that had never been done before. Aging a suspected killer over several years in drawings required an experienced forensic artist. The small voice in my head saying, "Julie, you are a gifted artist. You can do this," pushed through my hesitation.

"Do you know what he looked like when he was twenty-six?" I asked. Having lived in Wichita during most of the years when BTK was active, I didn't recall seeing early sketches of him on the news.

"We have several flip-book drawings we assembled from witness accounts, but we couldn't get a lead from them. We can only assume he's around forty-six now. You need to build a base for age twenty-six using the flipcharts, the cold case files, and witness interviews. We also have reports from psychiatrists who hypnotized survivors, and you can reinterview witnesses if you need more. Then we want to see what he looks like now at forty-six or forty-seven, with a full head of hair, bald, with and without glasses, and with and without a mustache. You'll have access to all the information we have, and we'll help where we can. Just let me know what you need."

"I need to know that my name will never be used in the news media as the artist. I have children to protect."

"I promise you, your name will never be used in conjunction with the investigation or the drawings. We'll refer to you as The Sketcher."

In the moment I accepted the assignment, I didn't understand how much the decision would change my life.

*A child's fear is a world whose dark corners are quite
unknown to grownup people; it has its sky and its abysses,
a sky without stars, abysses into which no light can ever
penetrate.*

~Julien Green

# Chapter 2

# Frightened Children

My first assignment was to familiarize myself with BTK's mode of operation. The first folder contained the brutal remnants of Joseph, Julie, Josey (Josephine), and the younger Joseph Otero's final days.

As I read the details and looked at the pictures, the last day of the Oteros' lives on January 15, 1974, took shape in my imagination.

Joseph and Julie Otero lived in an unassuming, tiny frame house on the corner of Edgemoor and 8th Streets in Wichita, Kansas, with their children Charley, Danny, Carmen, Josephine, and Joseph II. Joseph Senior wanted to be involved in aeronautical engineering in the Air Capital of the World and worked at Cook Airfield in Rose Hill, Kansas. Julie stayed at home with the kids after being laid off from her assembly line job at the Coleman Company. The five children attended school and were good students.

Their day began as an unremarkable, gray and cold Tuesday morning.

"Mama, what kind of sandwich did you make for me?" 11-year-old Josephine (Josie) Otero asked.

"Ham and cheese."

"No, I want peanut butter and jelly today," Josey whined.

"Too late, the ham and cheese are made."

"Ma-a-a-ma. The ham and cheese'll hold until tomorrow. I want peanut butter and jelly."

"You aren't hearing me, daughter. You will have ham and cheese."

"You don't *care* what I want!"

"Stop arguing with your mama," Papa told her. He had just returned home from taking Josie's older brothers and sister to school.

She hated it when Papa was home at this time of day. It was harder for her to win an argument with Mama when her parents were together. As this thought entered her head, the dog whined at the back door. Josie's nine-year-old brother, Joe, ran to the back door to let the dog outside. When he came back, a man was with him—a man they didn't know. A stranger with a gun.

"All I want is your car and some food."

"Take the car. Take what you want. Please don't hurt us," Papa pleaded.

Mama and Papa Otero shot glances of dread at each other, tamping down a growing panic, hiding it from Josie and young Joe.

"I want all of you to go the bedroom. Come on, let's go," the man ordered. The intruder forced them into Papa and Mama's bedroom and told them to lie down on the bed. He put little

Joseph on the floor.

I envisioned them praying silently that their captor only wanted their car, food, and money. They cooperated long enough for him to tie their hands and feet with Venetian blind cords.

Papa winced as the man tightened his bindings. "I was in a car accident and have some bruised ribs," Papa told him.

The intruder loosened the cords and put a coat under Papa's head. Perhaps their trespasser wouldn't harm them. In the aftermath, they might all be okay.

Mama and Papa formed muted "shhhh" sounds with their mouths to comfort Josie as the man bound her baby brother on the floor. "Don't say anything, don't make this guy mad" was their unspoken message. Josie remained calm.

The stranger hesitated after binding nine-year-old Joseph. For a few minutes he seemed unsure what to do next. Then, without warning, he produced a plastic bag and pulled it over Papa Otero's face. It stripped away the thin veneer of hope that this man would not harm them. Only raw panic remained. This was no longer an intruder; he was a monster from a nightmare… too awful to comprehend.

The attacker moved on to Mama, strangling her with a cord. Papa's struggles to breathe tore the plastic bag covering his face.

Josie watched in blind terror as the attacker returned to her Papa and strangled him with a cord. Josie's little brother lay on the floor at the foot of the bed, whimpering at the sounds of struggle taking place above him. The assailant placed a plastic bag over the little boy's head, but removed it when Mama regained consciousness and begged him to spare their son. The man then strangled Mama to death as Josie's thoughts locked in the consuming certainty that she was going to die.

He attempted to strangle Josie, pulling the cord tighter and tighter, denying her air. Despite his efforts, she revived in time to see him carry her brother into another room with a plastic bag over his head. He died with the stranger standing over him ... watching him suffocate.

When their attacker returned to find her conscious, he carried Josephine Otero to the basement, where he hung her by her neck from a beam. Only God and Josie know her final thoughts.

Finding sexual pleasure in killing her, the serial killer masturbated on her dead body.

Hours later, the three oldest children arrived home from school and discovered the gruesome scene of their murdered family.

The murders of Josie Otero and her family wove thick threads of fear and suspicion through the fabric of the community. It left Josie's three surviving siblings, Charlie, Danny, and Carmen, forever sorting through the tatters of their lives, attempting to find places in which to lock away the horror their family experienced. The mystery still endured in 1992, and it was my job to shed light on the man responsible.

# Chapter 3

# Julie

As I read the case file and drew mental pictures of the Oteros, the brutality of their final hours rekindled memories of my family during that time.

The oldest of eight children, I was barely a teenager when the four members of the Otero family died on January 15, 1974. My seven brothers weren't allowed to read about the killings. I could watch television news and read the news stories during my daily paper route. I told the boys the bare facts of the murders.

My 14-year-old imagination filled with Josephine Otero's thoughts as she was terrorized by the unknown assailant. They were my nightmares. I believed Josie's final words were a prayer to the Virgin Mary. I hoped it gave her solace. She was close to my age, and like me, she was a budding artist. Josie's world had been violated in the worst way imaginable. Her family and her life were taken from her. What remained for us to see were grainy black-and-white films on the news showing Josie's lifeless body carried from her home, her shroud a black plastic body bag.

My seven younger brothers and I were among the thousands of people haunted by this horrific tragedy. The thought that someone could walk into a house and kill people, that kids could die under such unholy circumstances, shattered our collective sense of security. Now we had a new reality. Death was real, unexpected, and it was possible for kids to die.

The day after the Otero murders was a bitterly cold day. The pervasively gray sky bled through the windows with a chill that etched despair on the day. My brothers and I were at home in our little house on Red Barn Street after school.

"I don't get it." Nine-year-old Danny interrupted my sketching. "Why does somebody kill kids?"

"'Cause he prob'ly hates 'em. He prob'ly stabbed them and cut them up into little pieces," Steve interjected in a successful attempt to scare the crap out of the youngest boys.

At 12, he was the oldest of my brothers.

I threw him a disapproving look, which he ignored.

Glancing at the front door, six-year-old Andrew was near tears. "Do you think he'll come here?"

Pulling himself to his greatest height, Steve told him, "Yeah, and he'll get you first 'cause you're the littlest and you can't run very fast!"

"CAN TOO!" Andrew believed his bluster would save him.

"Can NOT 'cause you're just a runt."

"SHUT UP!" I intervened. "There are eight of us and only one of him. He doesn't stand a chance in *our* house 'cause we'll dog pile on top of him. Right? So just settle down and quit talking scary crap."

Being the oldest and the designated babysitter gave me some advantages. Being the only girl diminished them. I had a few victories. This, however, was not one of them.

There was grudging but general agreement that I was right about us being able to gang up on a bad guy. We were the solid eight in that respect. We would stick together.

But Steve was in no frame of mind to settle down. "Just 'cause you're the oldest, you think you can tell us what to do!" He flew across the sofa at me, covering his fear with anger. "Well, you can't! You're not the boss of me."

"I am when Mom and Dad aren't here. They said so. So

there!" It was my best possible impression of a grownup as I protected my drawing tablet from his flailing arms and legs.

"I'm going outside" he declared when I dodged his attack.

"Me too!" echoed David, Brian, and Danny, the next three oldest boys after Steve.

"No way. You all have to stay in the house until Mom and Dad come home. They said so."

"Did not!" was the last angry outcry from whoever slammed the back door.

He was right; they had not said so. The unspoken truth? I was afraid for all of us. If the boys were inside the house, I felt I could protect them from whatever might happen. It was patently ridiculous, but at 14 I had illusions of being Super Girl, and it was my mission to protect my brothers. Sigh.

*Always an argument with these guys."*

I gritted my teeth and relented.

My younger brothers occupied themselves with their imaginations. Matt and Andrew, both quiet and loving little boys, built imaginative construction sites in the backyard with their well-worn, hand-me-down Tonka road grader and bulldozer. It reassured me to hear their childish banter, even their periodic swearing, while they created a building site for their imagined skyscraper. Their escape from the reality of our world was complete.

On the front porch, Paul, the youngest, created a happy fantasy family with his second-hand, beat-up Fisher Price jet plane flying to exotic places. His three-year-old voice making the sounds of a plane taking off worked magic on my outlook. The made-up conversations of his imaginary, contented family made me smile for the first time that day.

The others ignored my orders to stay in our yard and took off on their bikes for their usual haunts at friends' houses. At their ages, being with friends dulled the sharp edge of fear.

The episode with the older of my brothers left me anxious. If one of them told our parents they left the yard, there would be hell to pay. Mom and Dad both worked to keep a roof over our heads. There wasn't always enough food, but we had shelter. We were a "good" Catholic family. Mom had a kid nearly every year, it seemed, until she couldn't. They needed someone to care for the children, but they couldn't afford to pay a babysitter. I was the next best thing: the oldest and a girl. My parents believed all a girl was good for was housekeeping and taking care of the younger kids. They made me responsible for my brothers.

Dad and Mom had impossibly high standards. Given that the four oldest of my siblings completely ignored me, I was often in trouble. Although, most of the time, solidarity saved me. If anyone told on anyone else, we were all punished—me more severely than the boys because I was accountable for them.

I went back to the drawing of a horse I had started the day before. Horses were my specialty. Sketching blunted the abuse from with my parents for housekeeping or babysitting infractions. Drawing masked the loneliness and sense of being worthless. The only time my hobby hadn't covered for my parents' abuse was when I had been much younger, and they had punished me for the simple fact that I hadn't lived up to their dream of the perfect little girl. Nothing made that better.

My mom and dad's vision of me changed as I became a teen.

I was expected to be chief cook, housekeeper, and babysitter. Their verbal and physical discipline increased with my responsibilities. Art became my only refuge in times of stress. It was my redemption, at home and at school, the only thing I knew I could do well.

With the younger boys in the backyard and on the porch, and the older ones scattered in the neighborhood, I sat bundled up against the cold on the curb in front of our house, drawing furiously. I distracted myself with nearly eight drawings that day, all of them horses. Convinced I wasn't the perfect daughter, I applied myself to drawing the perfect horse.

The older boys returned to the house before Dad and Mom came home from work, and mercifully, none of my brothers mentioned leaving. We escaped a beating that day.

I read the *Wichita Eagle* on the evening of January 16, 1974, as I delivered newspapers. It reported that the murders of Joseph Sr., Julie, Josephine, and Joseph Otero II may have been related to Mr. Otero's work in Puerto Rico. I told my brothers. We held on to this prospect, hoping it was true. It was a thin hope, but it restored our sense of security. If true, it meant the crime wouldn't be repeated. What we didn't know was that the killing had only begun.

*Man can live about forty days without food,*
*about three days without water, about eight*
*minutes without air, but only for one second without hope.*
                                        ~Charles Darwin

# Chapter 4

# Courage

The next file contained the gory details of Kathryn Bright's murder and her brother Kevin's narrow escape on April 4, 1974. My mind filled with mental pictures of their day as I read their story and viewed the pictures in her cold case file, thinking that "cold" was an apt description.

Twenty-one-year-old Kathryn Bright and her 19-year-old brother Kevin arrived home that afternoon to find an unknown intruder waiting in a bedroom. The man told them he was wanted by police in California. All he wanted was a car and some money.

Fearful and skeptical of the man's story, Kathryn and Kevin followed their trespasser's orders and watched for opportunities to escape.

The stranger ordered Kevin to tie his sister to a chair and forced him into another bedroom, where he attempted to tie the young man to a bedpost. Filled with raw anger at this man, Kevin attacked. Only five-foot-six and 115 pounds, nevertheless, he caught the much taller and heavier intruder off guard. During the struggle, the man shot Kevin in his forehead. Kevin didn't remember the pain of the wound or passing out.

Kathryn was working at loosening her bindings, fighting to free herself, when she heard a gunshot. Her breath coming in desperate heaves, she pushed past her horror and was nearly free when the man came back to her room. He held a knotted cord in his hands and attempted to strangle her. She fought him with all her reserves, but she blacked out. I imagined her last conscious thought was, *I'm dying.*

Kevin regained consciousness and struggled to stand, spurred by the sounds of the fight taking place between his sister and her attacker. It was suddenly quiet. *Did Kathryn lose?* The bastard appeared in the doorway. Kevin threw himself at the man, adrenaline magnifying his waning strength. He saw the gun in the intruder's shoulder holster, grabbed it, and attempted to pull the trigger. Fueled by fear, Kevin's opponent wrestled the gun from Kevin and shot him a second time. The young man lost consciousness again.

Assuming Kevin was dead, the man returned to Kathryn's bedroom. She revived and took the offensive. She fought desperately to escape. He pulled a knife from his pocket. Ironically, she recognized it as a Boy Scout survival knife. Her brother had one. The pain she felt was searing ... blinding ... her world abruptly consumed with it. She wasn't conscious of her own screams. He stabbed her 11 times in the stomach. In the moment before passing out, she heard the front door slam. *Kevin escaped.*

Kevin awakened weak but determined. He summoned all his remaining strength and ran out the front door in search of help. He was the only victim to survive an attack by this serial killer.

Seeing one of his prey escape, the man realized he was in danger of capture. He picked up the few items he had brought with him and ran out the back door, leaving Kathryn Bright bleeding to death on her bedroom floor.

Kathryn was never a quitter. Slowly, painfully, she dragged herself to the living room and picked up the telephone to call for help. A neighbor, alerted by Kevin, called the police. The officers found her holding the phone in her hand, still breathing. She later succumbed to her wounds. Her final words were,

"I have no idea who did this to me."

⸙

Six months after the murder of Kathryn Bright, and Kevin Bright's narrow escape from death, a reporter with the *Wichita Eagle* received a phone call saying he would find information related to the Otero family murders in an envelope tucked inside a book at the city library. The letter was from someone claiming responsibility for the killings. It also contained a detailed description of the murder scene, along with photographs of the victims. The writer described himself as BTK, an acronym for Bind them, Torture them, and Kill them.

Wichita, Kansas, had a serial killer in its midst.

*Loneliness and the feeling of being unwanted*
*is the most terrible poverty.*

~Mother Teresa

## Chapter 5

# Refuge

Reading Kathryn Bright's case file led me back to late spring 1974. Her murder became a metaphor for my life. Back then, I was dying a slow and painful death from abuse, seclusion, and unhappiness. I felt that death would be a sweet release from the despair of my existence.

My spring days dragged inexorably toward summer. Each day brought me closer to another summer of isolation. I would be separated from school and from anyone who showed appreciation for my drawings. Sketching was my only escape from the slavery that was my life, from the wrenching fear of my father coming home and finding something… anything… wrong. The "anything wrong" was cause for punishment, and he always found something. He lined us up in the hallway and worked his way from the youngest to the oldest, gathering anger as he went—sometimes with a slap, always degrading us. Countless times, I saw my brothers lifted off their feet from one of his blows, their heads hitting the wall. He seemed to vent some deep-seated vengeance, intent on drawing blood.

I dreaded June, July, and August. During the school year, I was only responsible for my brothers after we came home from school. In summer I spent every day during the week as a full-time nanny, housekeeper, and cook and suffered the consequences for all mistakes. During the weekends, I worked as my mother's helper, my spirit enduring a slow death from my mother's contempt. My usual sanctuary—sketching—did little to ease my anguish.

A few days after summer "vacation" began, Grandma and Grandpa Riedel came to see us. They lived in Hays, Kansas, about 200 miles from us. I seldom saw them, but when they were in Wichita, my parents didn't beat us, and Grandma's laughter made our lives brighter. Anticipating their visit was the happiest I had been in a year. My brothers and I fed on each other's enthusiasm.

"Okay, guys, we only have a few hours to make the house spotless for Grandma and Grandpa. Let's split up the cleaning chores."

"I wanna help!" Three-year-old Paul pushed his way through the older boys.

"Come on, Paul, I'll teach you how to clean up a front porch." Steve, the oldest, took Paul's hand and led him outside.

"Danny, you and Brian wash the dishes," I ordered.

"Aw, come on, that's girls work. We don't wanna." Their complaints rang through the house.

I was too excited about Grandma and Grandpa coming to be mad at them. All I could manage was a scowl. "Okay, the rest of you go clean your rooms and get your junk out of the living room. GO!" I washed and dried the dishes and pulled out the vacuum cleaner.

Nine-year-old Matt appeared in the doorway. "Can I wipe the dirt off the tables?"

Behind Matt, always wanting to please, was Andrew, soon to be seven years old. "Me too. Can I?"

I provided each of them with a towel. "Just be careful with the glass stuff on the tables."

My words barely made the trip across the room before an ugly figurine of a lady in a swooping dress shattered on the floor. The boys' faces imitated deer in the headlights, silently asking, *How did that happen?*

I tried to ease their anxiety. It was an accident, but the fear of our parents' reaction overshadowed my reassurance. There would be hell to pay for this. All three of us knew it.

I swept the broken glass and finished cleaning the house, trying not to think of the price I would pay later.

Mom was always suspicious of me when I felt happy, and my enthusiasm at the prospect of seeing Grandma and Grandpa again put her on edge. She had been more critical than normal for several days. Confidant that I could make her feel better with a clean, tidy house, I doubled my efforts to make sure everything was right. But the broken trinket put her over the edge. "I can't trust you to do anything right. You can't even handle a couple of little boys." She slapped me several times, leaving deep red handprints on my face.

The boys escaped her wrath. The only good thing about that was my slim hope that Dad would be satisfied, and we wouldn't be subjected to one of his tirade-laden line-ups.

"You'll spend the rest of the day in your bedroom without dinner, and you'll stay home when we all go to the zoo on Sunday." Mother didn't mention the clean house.

*I tried so hard to make everything perfect for Grandma and Grandpa's visit. I tried so hard.*

Happiness has a short lifespan without encouragement. It turns to desperation in a heartbeat. Depression obliterated the remainder of the day. I didn't hear my grandparents arriving.

"Julie?" It was Grandma, sitting on the edge of my bed. I hadn't heard her come in. With my face turned away from her, she gently smoothed my hair. She rested her hand on my shoulder for a moment and carefully turned me toward her. My tear-swollen eyes and the still-red handprints on my face spoke volumes. "Come help me set the table for dinner, dear."

I stared at her, unmoving, fearful of leaving my room.

"It's okay. I told your mom I need you to help me, and you're gonna have dinner with us, too."

Grandma could always make things right. Whatever she said trumped my parents' anger. All I could think about was what would happen after my grandparents left. I would pay the price of my grandmother's kindness with a beating. I couldn't stand the thought of living like this anymore. Every good feeling that began to grow was immediately drowned in my parents' anger and retribution.

In the kitchen, gathering dishes for the table, I walked in a trance. I don't remember picking up the knife and putting it against my chest. I only recall Grandma snatching it from me. "Don't ever do that again." Her face reflected shock and concern as she put the knife away and pulled me into her arms. I hadn't felt that safe and loved since I had last seen her. She led me to my bedroom. "Stay here, I'll be back in a minute."

Sitting on the edge of my bed, waiting for what was next, I felt nothing: no fear, no sadness, no hope. I didn't look up when she came back. I flinched when she touched me. Human contact was a thing to fear.

She gently rubbed my arm to settle me. "Would you like to come stay with us for a while?" she asked.

Her words didn't register immediately. Completely absorbed in my desperation, I was unprepared for solace, unsure how to react to this offer of respite, fearful of the toll my dad would extract later.

I never learned why my dad allowed his parents to take me with them. The reasons didn't matter to me. During the drive from Wichita to Hays, Grandma and Grandpa tried to distract me with stories of when my dad was a little boy. The little boy in their tales bore no resemblance to the man who demeaned and beat me for the sole crime of disappointing him as a daughter. My parents would have no happy memories of me to share with my children. I stopped listening and slept the remainder of the trip.

My grandparents lived in a house that Grandpa built. It had a front porch with old metal chairs where Grandpa and I sat for hours in the evenings, watching far-off summer storms build against the backdrop of the West Kansas sunset. One evening a thunderstorm brewed close to the house and lightning struck nearby, leaving Grandpa's hair standing straight up. Normal people would have been horrified. He laughed; we both laughed. It was a tonic for my tattered soul.

I slowly came out of the fog that prevented me from seeing the goodness around me and fell into their routine. We puttered around the house during the mornings, fishing, cleaning, gardening, washing clothes, and preparing their farmer's lunch. The mid-day meal was a feast—the biggest meal of their day. Grandma served the vegetables and fruits she canned and stored in the cellar. Choosing the veggies and fruit for the noon meal made me feel part of their circle of love—trusted, protected, and wanted.

After lunch the three of us would drive around the

countryside, looking at farms. Grandma required us to be home in time to watch *As the World Turns*. I became a fan. The problems of the people in the soap opera became entertainment.

Grandma's sense of humor made everything fun. Her laughter rang through the house over some silly thing that happened, and my entire body would laugh with her. One afternoon I talked her into doing sit-ups with me. She thought the exercise was hilarious. We needed music, so I sang the Meow Mix cat food commercial. Her laughter was a thing of beauty, like a treasured song.

In the evening, we fished.

"You ever bait a hook before?" Grandpa asked me as he, Grandma, and I sat on a cliff over the edge of the water.

"Uh, no." My eyes widened at the thought.

"We're fishin' with worms today, and they're the hardest ones to put on yer hook. Okay, now grab the hook here." He demonstrated and I followed his direction. "Now reach in the can and pick up a worm."

"Ew!"

"No, no, no. Not like that, like this." He rolled his eyes, feigning frustration. "You are such a girl!" He laughed.

The poor worm was in a state of panic, flipping around as I held its mid-section.

*How can anyone put this thing on a hook?*

I was torn between setting it free and wanting with all my heart to make Grandpa proud.

"Here, baby, I'll show you." Grandma took my hook and worm. "You can't *tell* somebody how to bait a hook, you have to *show 'em.*" She gave Grandpa a look, pretending exasperation.

"You hold the hook like Grandpa said and pull the worm over it like this—" was as far as she went before she pricked her finger with the hook, lost her balance, and fell into the lake. She made a bigger splash than I would have predicted. When the water settled, there was nothing visible on the water but Grandma's broad-brimmed hat.

I was hysterical and ready to jump in and find her.

"Wait a second." Grandpa put his hand in front of me to keep me from jumping in.

"But she—" Before I completed the sentence, she surfaced, blowing a spout of water as her head cleared the water, laughing like it was the funniest thing she had ever done. She inhaled water, choked on it, and continued to laugh.

Pushing my fear aside, I laughed until my eyes were filled with tears. Not because it was comical but because Grandma exuded unfettered joy, and I felt it too. My conditioned first response to everything was fear that I would suffer for savoring a moment. Until that day I didn't understand how to experience enjoyment without the resulting dread of reprisal.

Grandpa succeeded in teaching me to bait a hook, although I was more successful casting the line and reeling in a fish. I couldn't abide killing and cleaning the fish, but he showed me how to do it. We went to a different fishing hole every day. Sometimes, we put our lines in at a small lake on the grounds of the old, decommissioned Walker Air Force Base, where we caught some of the biggest fish. Other times we went to a lake in Ellis, Kansas.

Driving home one day, we stopped on a road so Grandpa could look around. The road was completely shaded by trees.

The cool air from the tree cover was a welcome reprieve from the summer heat and signified a lovely, quiet time in my life.

We often went "visiting" to farms owned by other family members. I roamed the land around the houses, finding pleasure in the stillness and freedom.

Sometimes, in the afternoons, they took me to the A&W for a cooling root beer, and once a week, we ate at a Chinese restaurant. Often we played poker or canasta. Our routine had an easy rhythm to it. The only stress occurred when it looked like we might miss *As the World Turns*. When that happened, Grandma would speak in her best German, scolding Grandpa for making us late.

They spoke German during the rare times I heard them argue, but there was no rancor in their voices. It was the emotionally uncomplicated banter of two people who had shared a lifetime of experiences. They had earned the right to be cranky with each other without fracturing their relationship.

As the fall semester of school approached, my parents insisted I come back to Wichita. I dreaded returning, but the weeks in Hays had changed me. Grandma and Grandpa made me realize that people can be a family with dignity, encouragement, and love. That it's okay for a young girl to feel joy without fearing retribution. I didn't have that in my Wichita home, but now I knew it was possible. I looked to the future with hope for the first time, knowing that one day, I would leave my parents and never look back.

*The minute I heard my first love story, I started looking for you,*
*not knowing how blind that was. Lovers don't finally meet*
*somewhere.*
*They're in each other all along.*

~Rumi

## Chapter 6

# First Love

After living with my grandparents, life in Wichita had the grim sameness as before my reprieve. I delivered newspapers in the mornings and evenings, went to school, cared for my brothers, cooked, cleaned house, and absorbed the verbal and physical pain my parents dished out daily, but I was a different person from the broken teenager who had wanted to die a few months before. I looked forward to the future, to my art, college, and escaping my parent's home. And then I met Hutch. My two favorite memories of childhood are the ones Grandma and Grandpa Riedel and I made together, and Hutch.

---

As I left City Hall after reading the Kathryn Bright cold case files, the sun drenched the day like sparkling wine. It brought back the day I met Hutch in 1975. It came to me as clear as a spring day after a cleansing rain.

---

"Damnit." I fell off my bike when it hit a rock. April 28, 1975, editions of the *Wichita Eagle* scattered around me. My knee hurt like hell and bled all over my delivery bag. Some of the papers landed on the cover of the drawing tablet I always carried with me. "Damnit, damnit, damnit!" I couldn't finish my paper route in this condition, and most of the papers—the ones without blood on them—needed refolding.

*What a damned mess.*

My brother Steve would rant and rave for weeks, and he would use it on me when Mom and Dad weren't around. I'd lose credibility. It was technically his paper route, but we ran it together. Worse than that, if Dad got wind of it… well, my left ear was still swollen from his last smack.

"Are you hurt?" Jan Michael Vincent knelt in front of me. I recognized that handsome square jaw immediately. But this was Hutch, a handsome, square-jawed senior at Maize High School, who looked exactly like the popular television star. He was on the school football team and his grandparents lived in my neighborhood. He pulled a white terrycloth towel from his gym bag. "You need to hold still so I can wrap your leg."

His touch electrified me. I forced myself to stand still. "You don't understand," I said. "I have to refold and deliver all these papers or there'll be hell to pay. I mean, my dad will be really mad." I couldn't very well admit it was a younger brother who would be my tormentor. I also didn't want Hutch to think I used swear words all the time. Suddenly, I wanted to impress him more than I wanted to deliver newspapers or get home on time.

"I'll help. Did you draw these?" He had picked up my tablet and was flipping through the pages.

"Yeah, I like to draw." I blushed, suddenly embarrassed by my art.

"Wow, they're really good!"

"I'll take that."

"Thank you."

"What?"

"You're supposed to say thank you when someone gives you a compliment," he said with an impish grin.

"Thank you." I rolled my eyes and smiled for the first time.

"By the way, you have a nice smile. You should do it a lot."

At that point, my face was burning, brilliant red.

With my leg wrapped, he gathered the newspapers, and together, we refolded them. We walked my bike home, and he accompanied me on the rest of my paper route, carrying my delivery bag and helping me throw papers. We talked like we had known each other all our lives.

Newspapers all delivered, he smiled at me and said, "So, see you tomorrow?"

"Sure, see ya" was all I could manage. My stomach felt like it was full of butterflies. He was so beautiful and he said he would see me tomorrow. Pretty exciting stuff for a shy, inexperienced 16-year-old.

"By the way, my name's Hutch."

*Oh, good idea, introducing ourselves.*

"I'm Julie."

He waved goodbye to me from his grandparents' front porch.

I walked around in a dreamlike state.

Mom, of course, noticed. "What the hell do you have to smile about? Are you even paying attention to me?" she yelled, swatting me on the back of my head.

"I wasn't smiling about anything."

I didn't do a good job of convincing her. She grabbed my already swollen left ear and pulled. "Don't lie to me. I saw that stupid smile you had on your face."

"Julie's got a boyfriend, Julie's got a boyfriend. I saw!" Danny sang.

I gave him *the* look.

*Oh, crap, you little worm. Don't tell her that.*

"That's just what you need, a boyfriend." Mom was on this. I saw a gleam of satisfaction in her eyes. It gave her something else to use against me. "Exactly what you *don't* need! You don't pay attention as it is. You can forget about having a boyfriend until you do things right around here first."

*According to you, I've never done anything right in my life.*

I wished I could say the words out loud without getting a split lip for my indiscretion. Instead, I tried distracting her. "I'll start dinner."

"See if you can do it without messing it up. Make mac and cheese," she snapped, nodding toward the six blue boxes on the counter. She heard the boys fighting and left the room.

---

Hutch and I saw each other on my paper route for weeks. He went with me when I collected for subscriptions.

"Let's go to a movie. Ya think your folks will let you go?"

"I'll just *tell* them we're going." False courage talking.

"You think that'll fly?"

"I'll let you know."

*Now for the hard part.*

At home after dinner, Dad and Mom were in rare good moods.

"Hey, you guys remember Hutch?

"Yeah, what about him?" Dad continued reading his paper.

"Well, we wanna go to a movie Friday night."

Dad's face was inscrutable. "Okay, but Steve has to go with you."

"You mean like a chaperone?" I was incredulous.

*I'll do anything, just let me go.*

"Yeah, that or you don't go."

I found the idea of my brother going with us as a chaperone difficult to swallow, but Steve was thrilled. Hutch played running back for the Maize High School football team, and Steve was a huge fan.

Our dates were part date and part schmooze the brother for future dates. The system worked, and Steve kept any secrets when Dad and Mom pumped him for information.

I hid my happiness from my parents. They were suspicious of contentment and went to elaborate lengths to kill it.

Our infatuation gently morphed into love. Talking about our future together, we vowed to each other we would not have sex before marriage. We kept that vow.

---

"GET THE F*** OFFA ME!" someone yelled as they were thrown against the door of my police department "study room."

My mind jumped back to the present. I watched cops scramble outside the window to subdue the guy who had caused the fight, physically dragging him away as he screamed obscenities at them.

*Good grief! Okay, I'm awake here. Come on, Julie no more daydreaming, you have case files to read.*

# Chapter 7

# Shirley

The third case file contained crime scene photos and investigation results from the Shirley Vian Relford murder on March 17, 1977. Three years had gone by since the murder of Kathryn Bright.

The thought that Shirley Relford's three children witnessed their mother's torture and murder by BTK shook me to my foundations. Steven Relford, six years old, was the police's best witness and described what took place in the house. It aroused a fathomless fear in me for my own three children, and for the first time, I was afraid. The reality of putting my kids in danger settled on me. Remembering Ken Landwehr's assurances that my name wouldn't be used in conjunction with the case kept me calm.

The morning of March 17, 1977, 26-year-old Shirley Vian Relford was sick. After her husband left for work, she sent her son, six-year-old Steven, to the store for some soup to settle her upset stomach.

On his way home from the store, a man stopped the boy on the sidewalk. The man said he was a private detective looking for a woman and a child, whose pictures he showed to the youngster. The child didn't recognize the pictures, shook his head no, and went home. Inside, he put the canned soup in the kitchen. When the doorbell rang, six-year-old Steve raced his nine-year-old brother, Bud, to the front door. Steve won the race.

It was the "private detective," BTK. He pushed the door open and entered the house, startling Steve. The man closed the blinds in the living room, turned off the television, and pulled out a gun. Fear paralyzed Steve.

Shirley Relford came out of the bedroom, wearing her robe, her dark eyes reflecting how badly she felt. Her voice in the hall alerted Steve's siblings, Bud and Stephanie, that she was out of bed. They joined Steve, his mom, and the intruder in the hallway. The kids held onto their mom in fear of this unknown person with a gun.

BTK told their mother about a problem he had with sexual fantasies. He told her that if she would let him tie her up, everything would be okay. The children didn't know what any of that meant, but Shirley was nervous. The children sensed her fear and began crying.

The man forced them all into the bedroom and tried to bind the children. Terrified, they cried and struggled. Shirley begged him to not hurt her kids. To settle the children, she and the trespasser put them in the bathroom with blankets and toys. Shirley tried to reassure them, but they continued to cry. BTK tied one of the bathroom doors to the sink. The children heard something being pushed against the other door. They were trapped inside.

The children listened from inside the bathroom until Steve heard his mom throw up and heard her struggling with the man. Bud and Stephanie were screaming and crying, but together, the three of them were able to push open the door to their mom's bedroom enough to see her. Six-year-old Steve told BTK he was going to untie the rope from the sink and call the police.

"I'll blow your f***g head off." It sounded like the man was scared and mad that things weren't working out the way he planned.

BTK tied Shirley Vian Relford's feet and hands and strangled her with the remaining rope while her children watched in panic, shrieking and banging on the door. They heard someone ring the doorbell, learning later that it was the postman. The phone rang. BTK seemed confused and frightened. He packed some things in a case and left.

When the three kids forced opened the bathroom door, BTK was gone. Steven ran for help.

On January 31, 1978, the *Wichita Eagle* received a poem from BTK called "Shirley Locks," bemoaning that his fantasy hadn't been completed to his satisfaction.

The world wouldn't learn until 2005 that BTK's sexual fantasies about Shirley and his plan to murder the children had been interrupted by the postman at the door and the phone ringing. BTK didn't cut the phone lines as he did with his other murders. Rattled by the children screaming, and the additional distractions, he cleaned up quickly and left without harming the kids. Shirley was a random victim BTK chose when he was forced to bypass his intended mark, one of Shirley's neighbors, because the neighbor had company.

*Being deeply loved by someone gives you strength, while
loving someone deeply gives you courage.*

~Lao Tzu

# Chapter 8

# Love and Pain

The stark facts of Shirley Vian Relford's murder at the hands of BTK jogged my memory. I recalled drawing a parallel between the pattern of deaths from this vicious killer and the pattern of slow, spiritual death my brothers and I experienced at home. Hutch's love helped restore my hope for the future; his kindness and attention were my lifelines. At home I drowned daily in a cesspool of degradation and physical abuse.

I was a junior when Hutch graduated from high school and joined the Air Force. We wrote to each other often, recommitting ourselves to our future and our love. His declarations of love in his letters always surprised me. Someone loving me always seemed surreal.

With Hutch I felt certain we would love each other forever. I envisioned we were like my grandparents when they were young and in love—a special relationship that would last a lifetime.

At home my second life was the constant fear of reprisal from my parents for any and all mistakes, real or imagined. I successfully maintained distance between the two, not allowing life with my parents to pollute my life with Hutch. Bruises, split lips, and black eyes sustained at home were just clumsiness as far as anyone outside our home knew. It was believable enough to convince other family members and casual observers that we were an average family of active kids. The assumption was, yeah, our dad had a temper, but lots of people do.

The personal hell and emotional fallout each of my brothers and I endured left our lives in tatters just like the families of BTK's victims. Their families were murdered by BTK. Our spirits were murdered by our parents.

A few months after Hutch went to Illinois for basic training, Mom came into my room with a letter she said was from Hutch. "I'll read it to you."

*You have no right to open my letter.*

I was shocked and angry she had already opened it but unwilling to risk saying it.

"Alright, pay attention. He says he met another girl and is breaking up with you. It's over."

"He just gave me an Air Force ring a month ago! That's not true. Tell me it's not true, Mom." My breath caught between a sob and shock.

"It says so right here, so you'll just have to get used to it. You couldn't marry him anyway. He's not Catholic." Having delivered her news, she crumpled the letter.

"I want to see the letter."

"No. Just get used to it. He found somebody else." She left me no comfort and took the letter with her when she left my room.

I was devastated. My confidence in his love was as fragile as blown glass. Long ago my parents had convinced me I was unworthy. It was easy to believe Hutch didn't want me.

I went through the first stage of grief fairly quickly but became stuck in the second stage, anger.

*Hutch didn't honor the vows we made to each other. Why am I saving myself for marriage?*

Underage and looking for trouble, I went to a bar with friends, telling my parents we were at a movie. Tom introduced himself with some stupid line like, "Hey, girl, you're way pretty."

Here was the trouble I sought. I broke my vow of chastity with Tom and didn't see him again. A friend told me later he was married with two children.

I prayed that Dad and Mom wouldn't question me about the movie. My prayer was answered; they ignored me when I came home. Terrified of their reaction if they found out I'd had sex, I ignored the missed menstrual periods until I couldn't. I was around six months pregnant when I told my parents. Shock didn't begin to describe my surprise. They were uncharacteristically kind to me during that time. There were no physical assaults. However, my out-of-wedlock pregnancy brought shame to the family. I had broken the laws of the church and deserved to be punished, they told me.

"We can't let anyone know about this. You have to stay in your room. No church, no school, no friends."

Mom told the school and anyone else who asked that I had gone to live with relatives who needed my help. I would be back for the final semester of my senior year. My grades were good, and I had earned enough credits in my first two years for me take off the fall semester. I spent the three months before my baby was born in my bedroom with the door shut. I listened to records and sang along with the Doobie Brothers, the Beatles, Kansas, Chicago, the Ozark Mountain Dare Devils, Fleetwood Mac, Boston, and Peter Frampton. While I sang, I drew. Together they preserved my sanity.

Hutch came home on leave while I was pregnant. Mom let him talk to me.

The look on his face made me realize my mom had lied to me about the letter. He was devastated about my pregnancy and quietly told me he didn't want to see me again.

My mom had betrayed me. Her quest to prevent me from marrying a non-Catholic had succeeded. I fell for it because it was easy for me to believe no one wanted me. In turn I betrayed Hutch's faith in me. Once again I wanted to die, but my responsibility to the life growing inside me kept me going. The residual anger I felt at my mom became just another incident in a life filled with anger and disappointment. After a short time I couldn't distinguish it from all the rest.

I saw a doctor only a couple of times and didn't know what to expect during labor. The pain was wrenching. When I prayed to distract myself from it, my mom slapped me and told me to shut up. "The pain is your fault. You need to suffer for what you've done."

The slap is all I remember now of the birth. I heard my baby boy cry when he was born, before a nun carried him away to his adoptive parents. I had no choice except to sign the adoption papers. *There would be no bastards in the Riedel household.* As though my parents having the eight children born of their union in the face of God legitimized the torture they heaped on us.

As bitter, silent tears coursed down my face, I saw no future and no past, only the pain of not being allowed to hold my baby or smell his breath. It was the pain I deserved for what I had done.

The parallel between my parents' cruelty and the atrocities visited on the victims of BTK rolled over me like a suffocating, black cloud. BTK's brutality was a warp of the mind, causing the suffering and death of his 10 victims and spreading fear in the citizens of the Wichita area. My parents' viciousness was a contortion of their lives and souls. They drowned the spirits of their children and left us to live with a desolating sense of being unworthy, unloved, and filled with fear.

---

I left the detectives squad that day with a deep sadness in my heart.

# Chapter 9

# Nancy Jo Fox

Nancy Jo Fox's folder contained a description of the crime scene and photographs of her still body as it lay on her bed, bound at the ankles and hands. She had been strangled with a belt. The swelling of her face indicated she had been strangled and revived before she died. There was semen on her legs. The phone line had been cut and the intruder had entered the house through a broken window. As I read, I should have gained insights from the file to help me capture this man's appearance. But all I could do was imagine Nancy's horror when she encountered death at the hands of the BTK strangler. His face was a blank.

Nancy came home from her second job at Helzberg's Jewelry on the night of December 8, 1977. She opened her front door, set her purse on a nearby table, and locked the door. She was tired and looking forward to a good night's sleep but first needed to take the edge off her hunger. The stranger standing in her kitchen startled her. She froze in fear. For a fleeting moment she recognized him … a customer at the jewelry store, maybe?

She was nervous but controlled herself. Surely, this man meant her no real harm. The man tried to calm her with a story of his plight and smoking a cigarette with her. It calmed her a little. She must not have known the man was the BTK serial killer. He forced her into her bedroom and told her to undress in the bathroom. When she returned to the bedroom, the man forced her to lie down on the bed. Fear struck a sharp, dissonant cord inside her … panic building. He took off his belt and slowly wrapped it around her neck as she struggled and scratched him, desperately trying to escape. He pulled the belt tight enough, long enough, for her to pass out. She regained consciousness, thinking maybe he would be satisfied with his fantasy and leave her. He pulled the belt tighter. She fought harder. As she died, he masturbated on her.

At 8:20 the following morning, a police dispatcher received a call from a man saying, "Yes. You will find a homicide at Eight Forty-three South Pershing. Nancy Fox."

The dispatcher asked for confirmation. "Eight Forty-three South Pershing?"

"Yes, that's right." And the caller hung up.

Following up on calls made from the public phone, they discovered a fireman who made a call from that phone only moments after the BTK killer's call. The fireman saw the man but was traumatized by the knowledge that the man he had stood beside was the BTK strangler. He was unable to provide a description, even under hypnosis.

Police and FBI tried to analyze the 15 words spoken by the BTK killer on that day but found no clues to help in their investigation.

Twenty-five-year-old Nancy Jo Fox was a smart, beautiful, hard-working woman with a good sense of humor who died in terror.

On February 10, 1978, KAKE-TV in Wichita received a letter from BTK containing the driver's licenses of Shirley Vian Relford and Nancy Jo Fox and taking responsibility for both murders and for the killing of one unnamed victim. Investigations at the time of the murders had convinced police that the BTK strangler had killed Shirley and Nancy, and the driver's licenses and letter describing the crime scenes provided the proof.

In February 1978, Police Chief Richard LaMunyon announced the presence of a serial killer in the Wichita area and warned women of BTK's habit of cutting the phone lines of his victims.

*One who gains strength by overcoming obstacles*
*possesses the only strength which can overcome adversity.*
~Albert Schweitzer

## Chapter 10

# The Dream of College

I laid Nancy Jo Fox's cold case file carefully on the cold metal table.

Back in 1977, the news of her murder had hardly registered with me. When Nancy was killed, I had scarcely recovered from the birth and adoption of my baby boy. The last three months of my pregnancy had changed me. I came through the isolation with a serenity and certainty that only a Benedictine monk could understand. When I returned home from the hospital, I knew with conviction that I would leave my parents' home and go to college immediately after graduation in May.

First, I needed a car. It would give me the freedom to get away. I continued working and became obsessed with saving money. I paid my parents $60.00 a month from my meager salary, but the rest was mine, and I put away nearly all of it. It wasn't difficult. I simply went from home to school, to work, and back home again to begin my third job of corralling my brothers, cleaning, and cooking.

Returning to school for the final semester of my senior year at Bishop Carroll High School was a difficult transition.

"If anybody finds out about you having a kid, we'll know it came from you," Dad and Mom warned me.

Convinced that the worst beating of my life would be the consequence of telling anyone the truth, I maintained the story of helping a relative in another city during the last three months of the fall semester. Even Linda, my only friend, didn't know the truth. My secret was safe.

Linda already knew about our other best-kept secret.

One day my father was thrashing me with his belt for a now-unremembered infraction when we heard a knock at the front door. Answering the knock and not recognizing the couple and teenage girl on our doorstep, Dad was gruff. "What do you want?"

"We're Linda's parents. Julie's friend, Linda? Is everything okay? We heard someone screaming."

"Oh, yeah, my kid Julie, she fell down the stairs. She's a real klutz, ya know, and a drama queen, that one." His demeanor softened for effect.

"Is she okay? Does she need a doctor?"

"Like I said, she just fell down the stairs. Julie, come here. Let these folks know you're okay."

I did, and the ruse continued: we were all just really active kids, clumsy, klutzy, or uncoordinated. I was a drama queen and the boys … well, they just needed to man-up, grow some balls, and quit being sissies. The legacies were outward scars and emotional wounds too deep to heal.

"My mom and dad think your dad's beating you." Linda caught up with me after school one day.

"I told you I was just clumsy and fell down the stairs. I think maybe Brian tripped me when we were goofing around." I toed the family line. Linda looked dubious. I didn't offer anything else.

*Yeah, and I'm gonna get the hell out of there as soon as I graduate. The future doesn't hold any misery as great as living in that house. All I have to do is maintain the story just a little longer.*

My friend didn't ask again.

Before I graduated, a school counselor helped me submit a scholarship request along with some of my drawings to several colleges. I was encouraged by praise from my teachers and the awards I won for my art work during high school. The application earned me a coveted art scholarship to Notre Dame University.

"Two hundred fifty dollars a semester? That's it?" My dad scoffed when I told him about the scholarship. "It costs a whole hell of lot more than that, and we can't afford it."

"I can work while I go to school," I begged, risking injury.

"Like hell. You aren't even smart enough to go to college and sure as hell not smart enough to go to Notre Dame. Forget it."

I nearly opened my mouth to refute what he said, but I knew it would be a mistake. I slipped away to my bedroom.

*Like hell I'm not smart enough to go to Notre Dame. I'm going!*

I bought a Dodge Charger and insured it with my savings. Affording college by working part time would be a challenge, but I was determined.

Over the next few days, I secretly began packing to leave for the trip to South Bend, Indiana, knowing I would find my way once I arrived. I would get a job and share a cheap apartment with other students. I would eat rice and beans. I would overcome any obstacle to go to Notre Dame.

I planned to leave mid-morning while my parents were at work.

*Let them try to find me. I'm eighteen. They can't tell me what to do anymore.*

As I carried my last two suitcases to the car, Dad came home unexpectedly. "What the hell do you think you're doing?" he yelled as he tore my newly purchased suitcases out of my hands. "You're not going anywhere. I already told you. You're not smart enough to make it in college. PERIOD!" He continued yelling and threw my bags against the wall, breaking the latches. He grabbed me by my hair, dragged me to my bedroom, and threw me on the bed. For emphasis, he slammed the door when he left. I felt fortunate to be in one piece with my hair intact. I sat on my bed, staring out the window into the gloom of an uncertain future and grieving for my dead dream.

Dad returned a few minutes later with a hasp and a padlock and locked me in my bedroom, bellowing through the door, "Forget about college. You won't leave this house 'til you're married. You got that?"

I didn't answer his question. I cried tears of desperation until no more would come.

He took the lock off my door when he realized it wasn't practical to keep me under lock and key. They would miss the $60.00 a month I paid them for living there. If I didn't work, I couldn't pay them. Mom also needed me for chores and to take care of my youngest brothers when I was at home. Maintaining my serenity was more difficult after that, but my resolve to leave that poisoned household remained intact. I was also deeply committed to making a difference for my brothers but didn't have a clue how to begin. If I revealed the abuse, no one would believe it any more than they had believed it for the past 18 years, and the boys would be subjected to worse abuse. People on the outside looking in believed that my parents' stories about the injuries were plausible.

One day shortly after my failed attempt to leave, I came home from work to find 15-year-old Brian trapped in a corner at the base of the stairs. Dad was beating him with his fists.

"Little bastard! I'll teach you what happens when you don't listen to me!" Dad took another swing, landing his fist against Brian's face.

My brother's face was unrecognizable. Blood gushed from his nose and mouth and he was beyond crying; a faint whimper was all he could manage.

Something overwhelmed my fear of my father. "NO! Stop! NOW!" I ran between them. Dad's next blow was in full swing and landed on my mouth. My lip split and began bleeding.

In the instant I stepped between Dad and Brian, Dad's eyes switched from senseless rage to recognition of what he was doing. I suddenly realized his violence was blind, in every sense of the word. Our relationship changed forever.

There were no sweet moments of forgiveness, only his brief realization, and my brothers received fewer beatings thereafter. He tried desperately to make amends to me by buying me gifts. I rejected all of them. When Mom told me Dad was shocked and embarrassed that he had hit a girl, I could only stare at her in silence as though she was from another planet.

*What the hell. He smacks you around regularly and has never hesitated before to slap me hard and often.*

When I still wouldn't relent, she resorted to telling me she would punish me for the rest of my life if I didn't accept Dad's apologies.

*Oh no, Mom, I know why Dad was shocked. I challenged him, stood up for my brother. Dad realized he lost all his power over me; he could no longer terrorize me.*

During that summer, I continued to work full time at Doonan Truck and Equipment and save money. As the fall semester approached, I waited for a day when my parents were less angry than normal while giving them both a wide berth until I was ready to announce, "Mom, Dad? I enrolled at Schweiter Tech School today. I'll learn computer programming and accounting."

"I told you, you're not going to college," Dad reminded me.

"It's a trade school and I paid for it myself," I said to appease him. "I only go to school part time, so I'll still be here to help around the house," I said to appease Mom. "And I'll still be working at Doonan and paying you the sixty dollars a month room and board."

"Sixty dollars a month doesn't come close to paying for your room and board. But since you'll still be around to do your chores, it might be okay." Dad went back to reading his newspaper.

*At last, a small victory.*

The courses didn't fulfill my dream of studying art, but I knew I would be able to get a higher paying job after graduating.

Then I would go to Wichita State University later and study art.

That summer I started dating John Thimmesch. He seemed like a nice enough guy. I had worked with him at Doonan Truck before my pregnancy started to show the year before. We had liked each other from the first day we met. When I noticed him openly flirting with me, I saw him as my way out of the existence I had tolerated for 18 years. Mom and Dad accepted him because he was Catholic. He asked me to marry him. I agreed. I didn't realize my dream of becoming an artist was further from my reach than any time in my life, but I continued to draw and paint during rare free moments. It was the one thing in my life that provided stability and joy.

# Chapter 11

# The Killer Communicates

It was 105 degrees and windy outside, but it was too cold, dark, and unsettling in the interview room where I studied the crime files of the BTK strangler. Paper was scattered around me like grim remnants of a past that continued to haunt us in 1992.

"How's it going in here?" Ken Landwehr broke into my thoughts.

"So, BTK didn't kill anyone between January 1978 and April 1985?" I asked.

"Right. He communicated with us, though. He sent messages to the *Eagle* and KAKE-TV between January 1978 and August 1979. We were certain we would be able to identify him during that time. Serial killers have a deep psychological need for attention, but when they start communicating, they make mistakes. Let me know if you need anything." He closed the door, leaving me alone with my thoughts.

I was impatient to start the baseline drawing for the age progression of BTK. Reading cold case files took a toll on my emotions and exhausted me.

As I read more about BTK's communications, a sick feeling crept into my gut. His messages had not been released to the public for fear of panic or that it would entice him to kill again.

There was a 3" x 5" card, postmarked January 31, 1978, that

had been received by the *Wichita Eagle*. A perverted version of the poem "Goldilocks" was stamped on the card, using rubber-stamped letters. It began "SHIRLEY LOCKS SHIRLEY LOCKS, WILT THOUGH BE MINE," and referred to Shirley Vian Relford. BTK was obviously not a well-educated man. He was barely literate. The person who opened the envelope at the newspaper thought it was a Valentine's Day message and sent it to the department that handled classified ads.

Then, on Friday, February 10, 1978, since the first communication didn't get the response he wanted, the killer contacted KAKE-TV. A two-page, single-spaced letter arrived describing two murder scenes in detail. The envelope contained copies of Shirley Vian Relford's and Nancy Jo Fox's driver's licenses. The writer claimed responsibility for their deaths and for the murder of an unnamed victim. Investigators later learned the unidentified woman was Kathryn Bright. "How many people do I have to kill before I get my name in the paper or some national attention?" the writer asked. It was BTK, and he threatened to kill again.

Police Chief Richard LaMunyon held a press conference on the evening of February 10, 1978, announcing the presence of a serial killer at large in the Wichita area. After telling the city how this man described himself in the first communication received in 1974, LaMunyon said the BTK strangler had threatened to strike again. He went on to say that police had not publicized BTK's first letter because they hoped to prevent future killings. He said the police revealed BTK's messages when they saw the most recent letter to KAKE-TV and realized their first instinct—to keep the information from the public—had not deterred the killer.

I remembered the fallout from Chief LaMunyon's 1978 press conference telling Wichita that BTK cut the phone lines of his victims. It became common practice for single women to check their phone lines when they arrived home to ensure the line had not been cut. Fear hung over Wichita like a sickening yellow fog.

On April 28, 1978, police answered a routine burglary call to a home in the 600 block of South Pinecrest. An intruder had entered the house through a basement window. Sixty-three-year-old Anna Williams came home from a dance at 11 p.m. and found some of her clothes, jewelry, and $35 were missing. The only outward similarity to a BTK crime was that the phone line had been cut. The next day she received an envelope containing some of the items stolen from her home and a note telling her that BTK had been in her home. Angry and frustrated at being denied his victim, BTK sent an identical letter to KAKE-TV. That envelope also contained items taken from Anna's home the night of the burglary. The letter said he was sorry he had missed her, because he had intended to kill her.

*Sweet Jesus! How could anyone live with something like that?*

Police stayed in her home for several nights, expecting BTK to come back. He didn't. Filled with fear at the violation of her home and the threat on her life, Anna never returned to her house. She sold her home and moved to an unnamed city.

The "Ghostbusters" task force was created on June 15, 1979, to investigate the BTK murders and to review other murders in the area and around the world for similarities with those credited to BTK. Fifteen detectives and three lab specialists made up the group, in cooperation with the KBI and the FBI.

The task force team sent a copy of the December 1977 call that BTK made after the Nancy Jo Fox murder to a specialist in New York who had perfected a process for computer enhancement of recordings. BTK's voice had originally been recorded on a slow-speed tape recorder, and the quality of the sound was poor. The consultant enhanced the recording using the same techniques he used on the Watergate tapes and on police dispatcher recordings of calls received in Dallas after John Kennedy was assassinated.

On August 15, 1979, the police played the enhanced tape of the killer's voice on local television and radio stations. A tip line received more than 100 calls during the first day of the broadcasts. The tips generated no additional information to identify the BTK strangler, a major disappointment to investigators.

*My drawings of this rotten excuse for a human being may help in his capture. I'm going to make a difference.*

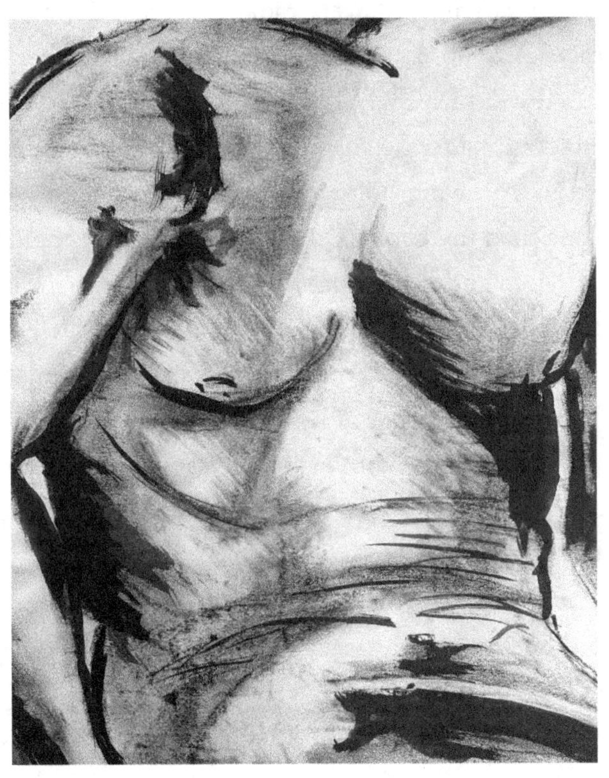

# Chapter 12
## Escape

I had trouble focusing on the BTK victim files of the murders committed when I was in my late teens. My mind drifted back to 1978.

While BTK was vying for attention during his communication binge, I had focused every minute of every day on planning my escape. Fear of my mom and dad had been as pervasive as Wichita's dread of BTK. Sitting back in the dilapidated metal chair, holding cold case files on my lap, I remembered being obsessed with leaving home but remembered there was more on the line than my personal safety. My brothers would pay the price for Mom and Dad's anger if I left without their "blessing." Marriage to a Catholic was the only option I could see.

John Thimmesch was handsome and charming and Catholic. I met him in the summer of 1977 before I was locked away for being pregnant. Along with everyone else, I thought he bought the story that I was out of town for three months helping a relative.

"What a great gal you are, Julie … helping out your cousin," John said one day after I returned to work in December 1977. Then he winked. He knew.

I frowned and said nothing.

Looking back on 1978, when John started "courting" me, I don't know if love played a role. But when he popped the question and I said, "Yes, I'll marry you," I knew it was a calculated move to get away from my parents. Whether it was love or divisiveness, I was determined to make it work. I would not have a marriage like my parents.

The wedding plans had a few hitches, but we dealt with them. Mom and Dad agreed to pay for the wedding. I had heard her and Dad talking about the expense of the wedding the night before.

As I was leaving for work, Mom stopped me. "I'm telling you this now. We aren't made of money, you know. So you tell the Thimmeschs to keep the invitations to a minimum. We aren't paying for every shirt-tail relative to come to this wedding."

"Yeah, I'll try to remember to do that." My sarcasm kicked in before I thought. Trying to placate her before she went after me, I came back with, "Mom, I know you and Dad are doing all you can for my wedding. I'll try to keep the expenses down." I was such a fraud … but a fraud with a plan.

"Just don't forget what I said."

*Okay, Mom, enough said. Don't beat the subject—or me—to death.*

Talking to John's parents about the cost of the wedding wasn't necessary. Tim and Joann Thimmesch were a considerate, loving couple whose first thought was about how expensive a wedding would be for my parents. Tim and Joann's sensitivity to the cost of our wedding was apparent the first day we talked about the ceremony. I wouldn't insult them by relaying any version of what my Mom said.

May 12, 1979, was the big day. John and I would exchange our vows of marriage at the St. Francis of Assisi church in Wichita, Kansas.

My wedding dress was beautiful, as were the flowers and church decorations. Regardless of my motives for getting married, it was going to be a pretty wedding and a happy day.

My dad and grandparents were with me in the dressing room at the church before the wedding. I was dressed, coiffured, and ready to walk down the aisle.

"You're such a pretty bride, child." Grandma beamed with pride.

"Yep, you're a keeper." Grandpa chimed in.

As Grandma hugged me, she added, "I'm happy to see you're marrying such a good man. I like John."

Their faces were aglow with happiness for John and me. They imagined us growing old together with the same love and respect they felt for each other.

Mom stormed into the room and, without warning, slapped my face hard.

*Dear God, what now?*

"I *told* you to not let those people invite more guests to this wedding, didn't I?"

She raised her hand to slap me again but Grandma intervened. "Enough!"

"You stay out of this. You're not paying for this wedding. Butt out," my mother snapped at her mother-in-law.

Grandma's surprised look wasn't lost on me. Had Mom ever talked to her like that before?

Turning to me again, Mom continued. "They invited five more people to the reception ... FIVE! Do they think we're made of money?"

I was in tears and couldn't speak to explain that those five people were on the original list of invitees but did not RSVP. Thinking that meant they wouldn't attend, John and I marked them off the list before Mom saw it. But the five guests decided to come at the last minute. I knew Mom well enough to realize an explanation would make no difference. It would only inspire another tirade. She was enraged and nothing would deter her.

*There are two hundred and fifty people coming to this wedding and she's bent out of shape about five more?*

For emphasis, she slammed the door on her way out. Dad left the room without a word.

Looking back on it, I wonder if my Mom slapped me in front of Dad to prevent him punishing her when he found out about the additional people. His punishments were brutal, up to and including throwing her down the stairs. Their relationship was perverse and dysfunctional.

"Come here, child." Grandma took my hand. "Let's fix your makeup and dry your eyes. You have a wedding to go to."

Grandma's efforts did little to lift my spirits.

I met Dad outside the sanctuary and prepared to walk down the aisle. He barely looked at me. The music began. I took his arm and walked with him to the altar, where he turned me, and his responsibility for me, over to John. There were no parting words or tender gestures from him. I didn't expect them.

*But why did he hate me?*

John and I exchanged our vows, his to love and protect, mine to love, honor, and obey. My face burned from the flaming handprint barely covered by makeup.

Our reception was held in the church basement. My most vivid memory of the occasion wasn't dancing with my new husband for the first time or throwing my wedding bouquet, it was of John disappearing from the reception and drinking himself into unconsciousness. He told me later that he couldn't handle the stress of the day. His embarrassed family put him in our car, and I drove us to our tiny rented wedding house in

Colwich, Kansas, a few miles outside Wichita. Whatever my hopes for a wedding night, they didn't include my new husband being in a drunken stupor. The good news remained: I was married and away from my parents. As I pulled our car into the driveway of *our* home, a sense of freedom washed over me. I imagined keeping house, cooking, washing, coming and going without the pervasive fear of being beaten.

*I'll make a home for us and go to college. Our marriage will be a good one.*

It was my new mission.

---

"I can't keep working at that place. It's too much. The stress is just too much. I quit," John announced as he walked in through the kitchen door on the third day of our marriage.

"What? What happened?" Except for the money we received as wedding gifts, which I hoped to save, we were poor as church mice. I couldn't imagine what would have inspired him to quit his job.

"Like I said, I quit. I quit my job."

"No, I mean, what happened to make you quit?"

"You didn't hear what I said? I can't handle the stress in that place."

"Uh, so, do you have a line on another job?"

"Nah, I'm gonna take a break for a while. I might take some temp work in construction. If I don't work for a while, we can live off what you make and the wedding money."

Stunned didn't begin to describe how I felt. My job as

activities director at the local nursing home didn't pay nearly enough for us to afford food and rent on the house. Our savings wouldn't last long, using it to supplement my income.

"A *break?* Seriously? What do you mean … how much of a break?"

"Leave it alone, Julie. I'm serious. Leave it alone."

I recognized that tone of voice and the glowering look on his face from the few times we had disagreed before we married. I knew it was a bad idea to push the subject, but he needed to understand how much we relied on his wages.

"John, we still need to eat and pay rent, and we can't do it with what I make."

"Use the damned wedding money and shut the hell up." He left the room.

I stood in the middle of our kitchen, wondering what to do next. John refused to eat dinner that evening in favor of a bottle of bourbon. By bedtime he was asleep on the couch.

*Okay, maybe he does need a break from working. I know he has trouble handling stress. I can work two jobs for a while until he gets past this.*

The pay in small towns is … well, small. My two jobs didn't make ends meet and we quickly spent our savings.

John made wooden furniture. I painted each piece with decorative scenes, and we sold them at flea markets and arts & crafts shows. The furniture John made and sold became his contribution to our household. However, the meager amount of money only paid for a joint with his buddies or whatever booze was cheapest. Working two jobs and painting furniture in my free time began to wear on me.

My dream of going to college was still alive. I wanted to learn how to be a serious artist, to earn my living with my art. How could our marriage fall apart so soon? We didn't talk about the future. We hardly spoke to each other.

I brought up the subject of college with John.

"You're working two jobs, and with taking care of our house and me. where do think you'll find time for college?"

"I saw in the newspaper that they're looking for carpenters at that new subdivision they're building here in Colwich."

"I see. So you not going to college is *my* fault? This is crap. College is your idea, not mine." His face reddened and he left the room, closing the conversation.

When we couldn't afford to continue paying the rent on the house in Colwich, we moved into a decrepit little house on Waco Street in Wichita, where the houses on the block were poorly maintained and cheap to rent. The sidewalks looked like a landfill of concrete slabs, and weed patches passed as front lawns.

One of John's aunts, Sharon Thimmesch, was an artist. During a chance meeting, this sweet lady offered to give me lessons in folk art. I accepted. I planned my grocery buying around the days of her art classes so John wouldn't be suspicious of my time away from home. Sharon's tutelage saved my sanity and kept alive my dream of being an artist.

"Hey, you remember Mark, my best man ... lives in Colorado now? He called me today." John met me at the back door after work. "Says he has a job for me in Denver if I can get there next week."

"Wow, that's great. Uh, what's the pay?"

"Is that all you ever think about—money?"

"I'm sorry, forget about that. When do we need to leave?" I was the perfectly programmed wife for John. Having lived my entire life believing I was responsible for everyone's anger, I easily accepted responsibility for John's and defused it whenever possible.

***

We moved out of the house on Waco with as many of our belongings as would fit into our old, forest green and white Thunderbird. We left everything else with my parents.

Driving through the open spaces of western Kansas toward Colorado exhilarated us and inspired our collective sense of possibilities. We felt free of responsibilities. The open road led to adventure and a new world for us. John had a light in his eyes I had never seen before.

Just outside of Russell, Kansas, reality struck. The engine of the Thunderbird died and, along with it, our euphoria. We had only enough money to pay for gas and food for the remainder of the trip to Denver. Repairing the engine on our Thunderbird was not possible. We were trapped in Russell, Kansas.

We needed help, and a call to my grandparents brought them to us. They drove the 30 miles to Russell and took us home with them to nearby Hays, Kansas, where we stayed for two weeks while we decided our next move. I wish I could have enjoyed seeing Grandma and Grandpa again, but our situation and John's disappointment made it impossible. John's call to his friend in Denver brought more bad news. The job in Colorado was no longer available. We needed to go back to Wichita, but first we had to earn money for the trip.

With what remained of our money, we were able to rent a mobile home in Hays. Grandpa gave us a faded old pickup truck to drive. John couldn't find a job he felt he could live with. In addition to working part time at MacDonald's, I found a full-time job on the assembly line at the Baxter Travenol factory, where I worked for the six months we lived in Hays, believing we would soon save enough for our trip to Wichita. John continued to drink. He was depressed because he couldn't find the right job so he could be the breadwinner. I was the sympathetic new wife.

"Julie, you won't believe this." John met me at the door with a smile and a gleam in his eye. "I have a job offer at Doonan Truck and Equipment in Great Bend."

"Okay, then. I think we can make it that far with our limping old beater of a truck, but where will we live?"

"I told my boss we're broke. He said we could live with him and his wife for a while."

Living with people I didn't know wasn't something I preferred, but we didn't have another option. We were barely surviving in Hays. We needed to move on, and in this scenario, John would have a job. The thought that he would be working for the same company where he quit his job three days after our wedding troubled me. Not enough to make an issue of it, but the thought took root.

Living with John's boss and his wife allowed us to save enough money to get a place of our own and begin saving money to move back to Wichita. I also put aside enough to pay for my tuition at Barton County Community College, knowing education would improve my ability to get a better-paying job.

"You just don't know when to quit, do you?" Was John's reaction to my announcement that I had enrolled in classes. "Three hundred and forty-eight dollars for a couple of classes?" He towered over me, red faced and angry.

"Yeah, but it'll make it possible for me to make more money after I take the computer classes."

"It better get you enough to take us back to Wichita. I'm not paying for any more college for you, and I'm not talking to you about this anymore. You got that?"

I waited for the first slap. It didn't come. I breathed a little easier.

*Oh, my God, he sounds like my dad.*

I recognized the abuser in John and the enabler in myself, but there was a threat of danger in how I handled it. I had to be careful. It didn't occur to me to counter his "I'm not paying for any more college" with "You didn't pay for it, I did!" Fear and caution ruled my response.

On June 15, 1981, the skies opened up and dropped 20 inches of rain on Great Bend in 12 hours, causing Barton Creek to flood and inundate this agricultural heartland town of 16,000 souls. We watched in fearful wonderment as water crept up the windows of our duplex apartment, fish swam past, and coffins from a nearby cemetery floated by our duplex. It gave the appearance of living in a dry fishbowl while the world around us filled with water. We placed as many of our things as possible on the kitchen countertops, hoping they would remain above the waterline, then we made it to high ground and waited for the water to recede. We lost most of our scant belongings. Not being insured, we lived with nothing until we could replace our drowned furnishings with a few pieces of used furniture.

The upside to being dirt poor is that when disaster strikes, you have fewer things to replace. I bought a rickety dining table for $10.00. Instead of appreciating the bargain, John reminded me that the money I paid for my classes would have set us up again with good furniture. All I could see was the loss of our photographs and my artwork, which were irreplaceable. I grieved for my drawings—so many memories gone.

We cleaned up the duplex after the flood and began the process of replacing furniture and household items. Then the other shoe dropped, this time at Doonan Truck and Equipment. John lost his job for being high at work. Another blow. How much more of this could we take?

John wanted to work outside and signed on with an oil-field crew. I prayed this would be the sort of work he liked and we would be able to save enough for our move home, but we continued to barely survive.

When the phone rang one afternoon in mid-November 1982, about a month after John began work in the oil field, I expected it be a bill collector.

"Mrs. Thimmesch?"

I heaved a deep sigh.

*Here it comes. Who do we owe now?*

"Yes, this is Julie Thimmesch."

"Ma'am, your husband had an accident. He fell off an oil rig."

"Is he okay?" I felt I was sinking in quicksand.

"Don't know, ma'am. He's at the big new hospital. You know where that is?"

"I'll find it." I didn't thank the man for notifying me. It was hard to focus on niceties. I would have prayed for intervention, but how could God have not seen what we were going through? I felt He had abandoned us.

Central Kansas Medical Center was bright and as shiny as a new penny. John was in the emergency room. He had three broken vertebrae and wasn't able to walk.

"We can operate and fix the damage by fusing the vertebrae using bone from his pelvis," a surgeon explained. "It's his best chance to resume normal activity. But his recovery will take some time."

"What does that mean ... take some time?"

"Recovery from this type of injury can take as much as a year before he can go back to work, and recovery is painful. We can give him medication for the pain, but he'll need to be dedicated to his physical therapy for a full recovery."

After John came home, my mom drove to Great Bend for a day to help. Her idea of helping was telling me how stupid I was for allowing myself to be so poor and to complain about John's family for not coming to our aid. When she discovered I walked to work because we couldn't afford to pay $5.00 to repair the flat tire on our car, she slapped me for the way I handled our "situation." When she slapped me a second time, I decided we were better off without her brand of help. I would reject any future offers from her. Too many memories of childhood competed with the challenges of what we were going through at the moment.

Mom left that day. I stood watching her drive away, thanking God she had come for only a day.

As the months of John's recovery wore on, he became angrier, and our marriage suffered further damage. There was little said by either of us that didn't result in anger and hurt feelings. John's pain became more difficult to control, requiring higher doses of pain meds, but he diligently worked on his physical therapy.

I was able to get a job in the office at an oil company, thanks to the classes I took at Barton County College, and I supplemented our income with a second job at a packing plant. We lived in constant danger of being broke.

Less than a year after the accident, John was mobile and his recovery complete. He greeted me at the door with, "You aren't gonna believe this. I ran into this guy I met at jobs placement… Lou Stephenson? He wants to train me to be a land surveyor."

"Can you do that with your back problem?"

"Yeah. Yeah, I only have to lift fairly lightweight equipment, and I can work outside. Don't even think about asking me what I'll make. Anything will be better than what I'm making now."

"Okay, so when do you start?"

"Tomorrow."

Relief washed over me. The job sounded tailor made for John. He could work outside, there would be light lifting, and we would have another salary coming in. I might be able to quit one of my jobs and spend some time sketching and painting again. Instead, I continued working two jobs to save money, though we never seemed to accumulate enough for a move home.

When I discovered I was pregnant, the expense of a new baby kept me working both jobs. The news of the baby gave us a new bond, but John continued to drink heavily and take pain medication. I feared for his life and our future but avoided saying anything to anger him. I didn't want to disturb the thin veneer of happiness we laid down with news of my pregnancy and his new job offer.

*Let the glue dry and then test it.*

The surveyor job lasted about a year until John injured his back again lifting a box of equipment. He needed another surgery to strengthen the bone of the previously injured vertebrae. John was prescribed bed rest and more pain medication until the day of the surgery.

Working a full-time job and a part-time job, dealing with the final month of pregnancy and caring for John seemed more than I could handle. I was bone tired.

On November 22, 1982, I went into labor. John and I played card games at home to distract me from the early labor pains. Finally, in pain the entire time, John drove me to the hospital. We had almost waited too long. Our son, John Thimmesch Jr., was born two hours after we arrived at the medical center.

Everything about my life seemed to move at breakneck speed with little time to react. The next day, John was able to drive me home. He held our sweet-natured baby boy, Johnny, cooing and smiling at him, while I made our first Thanksgiving dinner as a family of three. He was smitten with Johnny, this small bundle of sleeping child. Aside from all of us being exhausted, it was a good day, better than any in the recent history of our marriage.

John's second back surgery was scheduled for the month

after John Jr. was born. The operation was a success, and two weeks later, an ambulance delivered John home. He was in a body cast, had a bad attitude toward his rehabilitation, and the pain meds only dulled his discomfort. He was in constant pain and needed almost continual attention.

Johnny united John and me, and he helped us to set aside all the events that had driven a wedge between us during the previous three years. Our love for him unified us as a family. Whatever sacrifices I made were no longer for me or John or our marriage; they were done for the love of this new life.

We couldn't afford to pay for a babysitter when I returned to work, so we used a variation of the plan we used after John's first surgery. We left Johnny with a friend who offered to watch him for no pay, and alternated it with times John could watch the baby. When John watched our baby, I arranged all the supplies and John's medication and food so it was within John's reach on the living room floor, and I put Johnny on a baby blanket nearby. John's ability to lift was limited to 5 pounds, and Johnny weighed 9 pounds 11 ounces when he was born. John could easily care for Johnny on the floor without lifting him.

My husband was besotted with our son. Most days when I came home, I found him lying on the floor with Johnny on his chest, talking to his baby boy in a soft voice or taking father-and-son naps together.

One Thursday evening after doctors removed John's body cast, he yelled, "Julie! Look at this!" He handed me a plain-looking envelope with a clear plastic window with our address showing through.

I grasped the paper inside and hesitated, looking up at John.

"Go ahead. Look." He was excited, but his face didn't betray much else.

It was a cashier's check for $25,000 from the oil company John had been working for when he fell from the rig. It didn't register in my brain. I looked back at John, thinking I had misread it.

"It's a settlement check for my accident. Remember when that lawyer talked to us after the accident?"

I shook my head no. It had been two and a half years since the accident. "Oh, wait. Yeah, I *do* remember now. He said he would sue the company and you'd get a settlement from them."

"And we didn't believe anything he said. We just signed and he left, remember? Well, look at it … it's twenty-five thousand dollars! We can move home."

Altogether, we had struggled to survive in Hays and Great Bend, Kansas, for four years—and now we were going home.

John announced, "Tomorrow, I'm going to buy a brand-new truck."

---

"Hey, Julie? Julie? Earth to Julie!" Ken Landwehr's voice yanked me back from Great Bend, Kansas, to the musty interview room where I was holding a pile of investigative notes about BTK. I looked at the clock.

*Good grief, I've been daydreaming for over an hour… gotta get back to work.*

"What's up, Ken?"

## Chapter 13

# Three Murders and The Faceless Man

The information in Marine Hedge's file read like a laundry list stated in clear terms without emotion and with no sense of the victim other than the facts of her death. But, having experienced terror for myself, I could imagine what she felt.

On Saturday, April 27, 1985, Marine Hedge didn't show up for her second-shift job at the Wesley Hospital coffee shop where she worked. According to friends and associates, she was a conscientious woman. Missing work without notice wasn't in her nature. Not being able to get in contact with Marine, her manager called the police to report her missing.

When Park City police drove by Marine's house, they discovered her driveway was empty. Her 1976 Monte Carlo was missing. Checking the outside of her home, they discovered her phone line had been cut. She was listed as a missing person, but the cut phone line was suspicious. The next day, her purse was found in a ditch. Her identification cards were missing. Marine's family prayed she would be found alive and unharmed.

On May 2 a patrol officer found Marine's Monte Carlo abandoned. There was a blanket and a bedspread in the backseat; the tires were covered with mud and leaves. On May 5 her nude body was found in a culvert seven miles from her home. Although police found a knotted pair of pantyhose beside her body, the autopsy confirmed someone had strangled her with their hands.

Investigators reconstructed Marine's last hours. They interviewed her old friend who drove her home from bingo and stayed with her until 1 a.m. on April 27. The investigation of her bedroom indicated she was probably strangled there sometime during the morning of April 27. Her bed showed signs of a struggle. This kind, sensitive, 53 year-old mother and grandmother had been murdered and stripped naked, her nightgown and underwear tossed aside on the floor. Similarities to BTK were present, but moving and dumping the body was not part of his previous murders. All of Marine's acquaintances and neighbors were investigated for potential motives and compared with similar lists from confirmed BTK victims, searching for matching names. There were no suspects. Investigators weren't certain she had been murdered by BTK.

I went to bed the night after reading Marine's files, filled with unanswered questions about her seven-year-old murder. There must be something or someone common among BTK's victims, perhaps a person all of them knew or worked with or lived near. The Ghostbusters task force investigated everyone associated with the victims. They used the newest scientific discovery of the time—DNA analysis—to narrow the suspect pool. Investigators on the task force studied similar victims in other cities. Nothing led them to BTK.

The next day found me back in the glassed-in room at the Wichita detectives squad, where the air was warm, humid, and heavy with the latest crime drama. The table was filled with BTK cold case files, and the smell of old paper left an acrid taste in my mouth. Worn down by the victims' suffering, I needed to give this killer a face.

Two more files to study before I could begin. I recalled the news of Vicki Wegerle's murder when she died on September 16, 1986. Bill Wegerle, Vicki's husband, had been the only suspect, so why was this file among the BTK cold case files?

Vicki's husband, Bill, drove home for lunch that Tuesday in September. As he neared his house, he saw his wife's 1978, gold Monte Carlo coming toward him, but he couldn't clearly see the driver. Arriving at the house, the first thing he noticed was the slightly ajar front door. Entering the house, he found the couples' one year-old son, Brandon, sitting on the floor. The toddler was crying. Bill settled their son and searched the house for his wife. He found her on the bedroom floor, unconscious and not breathing, her ankles and wrists tied with a cord. He called an ambulance. His beloved wife was beyond the help of the dedicated fire rescue and EMTs. After arriving at the hospital, Vicki Wegerle was pronounced dead. The autopsy determined she had been strangled with a nylon stocking. The investigation showed her driver's license missing from the house. Police found skin under her fingernails and tested over a thousand men, trying to match the evidence to the killer but with no luck.

An arctic chill ran down my back as read the file describing the February 1, 1991, strangulation of Delores Davis. Her body was found in a ditch east of Wichita in Sedgwick County. She had been missing for 13 days but died on January 19, 1991, the day she disappeared. The cold facts included her height, 5' 5", and weight, 130 pounds. She was an attractive, 62-year-old single woman who was tied up, strangled with pantyhose, and her body dumped and posed in rural Sedgwick County near a river. A plastic mask lay near her head. Police found her car in her driveway; her car keys had been thrown onto the roof of the house. Her killer had thrown a cement block through the sliding glass door to gain access to the house and had ransacked the drawers in her bedroom, taking costume jewelry and her purse. Her phone line had been cut.

I stopped Ken Landwehr as I left for the day.

"Why are Marine Hedge's, Vicki Wegerle's, and Delores Davis's cold case files in with the other BTK files? I thought Bill Wegerle was the main suspect in Vicki's murder, and I don't remember hearing about Marine and Delores in connection with BTK."

"There are two major differences with the Marine Hedge and Delores Davis cases. Both were killed by manual strangulation and their bodies moved from where they were killed and dumped in a ditch. BTK didn't use those methods with his other victims. The similarities to BTK's other crimes—the phone lines being cut and his method of entry—weren't enough to convince investigators. Those differences set up a lot of doubt, but I believe they were killed by BTK."

"And Vicki Wegerle?"

"There are several cops who still believe Bill murdered his wife. To all appearances, he loved his wife and they were a happy family. We're still suspicious of Bill—he failed two lie detector tests—but we couldn't establish a motive. Similarities to BTK in each case are enough for us to keep those files active as part of the BTK investigation."

I was edgy as I drove home that night. I was afraid for my children if my name was linked to the drawings I would soon begin and was afraid for my sanity if I didn't. These victims were a part of me now. I couldn't abandon them.

---

That night, I had *The Nightmare* for the first time. The attacker in my dream had no facial features and was silent while he covered my head with a plastic bag and wrapped a nylon stocking around my neck, pulling it tighter and tighter until I awoke gasping for air. I identified with BTKs victims, having been a target of tyranny most of my life and, many times, in fear for my life. Now a new horror—the BTK murders—infected me. Variations of the nightmare came to me often; his face was always a blank.

Walking across the grocery store parking lot the following day, I saw a faceless man in my peripheral vision. I knew it was time to begin building BTK's face.

# Chapter 14

# Family and College

I finished researching the BTK murder files the end of July 1991. The next day, I would begin building BTK's appearance when he was 26 years old. I woke at 2 a.m. from after another bout with *The Nightmare* of the faceless BTK killer. I wandered through the house, checking the locks on doors and windows. I looked in on the children before settling at the kitchen table. John was asleep on the couch again. The wind was ferocious, setting up symphonies of eerie dissonance as it blew through trees and along the house siding, stirring my already fractured imagination. The dark room held shadows formed by the ambient light. As the wind died, silence filled the house.

My mind drifted back to when John, Johnny, and I moved back to Wichita from Great Bend in 1984.

The settlement money from the oil company allowed John to buy a new pickup truck and provided us with enough to buy a small house in Orchard Park, a subdivision in Wichita. I took care of other people's children in our home during the day so I could stay home with Johnny. John made benches, small tables, and cabinets, and I painted them. I sold some of my paintings, and John had a paper route. Our odd jobs and the remaining settlement money kept us solvent.

John continued to drink himself into a stupor almost daily. The more he drank, the worse his anger and disdain for me became. Talking to him about the problem only made it worse until I gave up and made myself responsible for keeping his anger under control. I simply avoided anything that might make him mad, including any discussion about college. I would wait before going to college. At the time, I needed to make my marriage work for Johnny. John didn't wield his anger against Johnny. Johnny's love for his father was the only reason I made the effort to keep our marriage alive. John and Johnny were a mutual admiration society.

In August 1987, when Johnny was five, I realized I was pregnant again. John's attitude improved toward me. He controlled his anger, but he continued to make cutting remarks about everything I did. It stirred memories of my father. Nothing I did was good enough for John.

John was excited and happy about having another child, and five-year-old Johnny thought it was "way cool" that he would have a baby brother or sister to play with him. Their happiness about the new baby helped us hold our marriage together.

The pregnancy was easy, but like Johnny, this baby was in a rush to be born. During breakfast on May 7, 1988, I announced it was time. Driving through rush hour traffic delayed us, and our baby's head crowned while we were in the hospital elevator. Nurses and doctors rushed to my aid. Jessica was 9 pounds 7 ounces of the most beautiful baby girl on the planet. In a moment's time I had another powerful reason to go back to school and to make our marriage work—mutually exclusive goals.

John drove me home the day after Jessica was born. I felt a budding sense of happiness with our little family of four. "John, what's with all the cars in the driveway?" I asked as we parked in front of the house.

"Oh yeah, some friends came over."

"I'm pretty tired. I don't really feel like having company right now."

"Well, no problem then, 'cause they're *my* friends. You don't have to entertain them."

My welcoming committee was a group of John's buddies playing loud music and trying to talk over it. Some of the "company" had large barking dogs with them, adding to the cacophony. The strong smell of marijuana wafted through the rooms. In my arms, Jessica startled and cried.

I put the baby in her crib in our room and Johnny in his room for a nap and confronted my husband. "John, you know I don't want our kids exposed to marijuana smoke. I thought we agreed on that."

Johnny had been there the entire time, inhaling that crap.

"I'm not throwing my friends out just because you don't like the smoke!"

"It's not me, it's the kids. This crap isn't good for them" I said, trying to appeal to his sense of responsibility to our children.

"Then open the windows so it blows outside if you're so worried."

My barely sprouted sense of well-being withered and died. "Can you at least get them to turn down the music and control their dogs?"

"NO! Go shut yourself up in the bedroom if you don't like it. The kids will get used to the noise. You're the only one who's bitching about it."

*That damned noise penetrates the entire house.*

I was angry but too tired to push the subject, and with his friends there, John would be even more stubborn about any hint of me telling him what to do. He would escalate the argument, and I wasn't prepared to face where it would lead. I opened the windows, gathered Johnny in my arms from his room, and we closed ourselves in the bedroom with Jessica.

I tried settling them with a lullaby. "Hush, little baby, don't say a word, Papa's gonna buy you a mockingbird. And if that mockingbird don't sing, Papa's gonna buy you a diamond ring."

It couldn't compete with the concussive music coming from the living room. I held Johnny in one arm and Jessica with the other until they both eventually slept.

---

I continued to babysit and sell my paintings and John's furniture and cabinets at craft sales until one day I could no longer tolerate being trapped in this pit of odd jobs and poverty. I had a hole in my life that only an education would fill. I talked about my dream of going to college with John's brother, Tim, who was my only confidant about my drive to attend school.

"This is something you need, Julie. For yourself and the kids' futures. I say go for it. There's all kinds of help out there for people who can't afford the tuition. I think you could even get free babysitting for your kids at WSU."

Tim's encouragement pushed me to investigate the possibilities. I spent the next few months making phone calls and trips to WSU, gathering the information and forms that would be my ticket to start classes the spring semester of 1989. Tim was right. I was eligible for grants and loans that would pay for tuition and books and for a housing supplement. Daycare for Johnny and Jessica was provided free at WSU.

"Hey, John, I fixed baked beans and the grill is ready to cook some steaks." I hoped cooking his favorite foods would set the stage for a good mood.

"Okay. Did you burn the beans like last time?"

I took a deep breath. "I watched pretty close this time."

Johnny and Jessica were fed and sleeping. It was just the two of us with no interruptions. "So how did the paper route go today?"

"Okay, what the hell do you want? Just spit it out."

I had lost the battle before the first volley. "I need to talk to you about what I did today."

"And?"

"I enrolled in classes at WSU."

"You enrolled in classes at WSU! You just don't get it, do you? I told you a long time ago, no more talk about college. PERIOD. I'm not paying for it."

"I applied for grants and student loans—which they gave me—and we get a housing allowance because we don't have much money. And the kids can go to daycare at WSU for free when I'm in classes." I stopped to breathe.

"Do you even know that the loans have to be paid back?" His face was reddening. He stood up, ready to leave the room and this conversation.

"John, listen to me, please. When I graduate, I can earn enough money to pay off the loans *and* still help us live better."

"So you're saying what I make isn't good enough for you? All you ever think about is money. If you can't be happy with what we have now, maybe you should just leave."

*Oh dear God. Have you been paying any attention at all to how we have lived the past ten years, not to mention who worked most of the time?*

"Me getting a college degree is better for all of us."

*I swear to God, if you say I'm not smart enough, I'll deck you.*

I kept that comment to myself.

"You're not going and that's final." He left the room.

*This isn't the end of it. You'll have to get used to me going to school, John.*

I continued planning for the first day of school, buying school books and supplies, which I hid in a closet, and enrolling the kids in daycare. Like all of the unsolved problems in our marriage, John and I didn't talk about it again. We returned to our daily routine. He ran his paper route, I babysat; he built furniture and I painted it, all the while watching the balance of the settlement money deplete.

The first day of school arrived. I expected an apocalypse with John.

"Where are you and the kids going?" John asked from the couch were he and his bottle of bourbon had slept the night before.

"To Wichita State University. My classes start today."

*Here it comes.*

He sat on the edge of the couch, leaning over his lap, head nearly between his legs, elbows resting on his legs. He slowly glared up at me, nostrils flared, but he said nothing. I looked him in the eye and let him know, "Jessica will be in daycare at WSU all day. I'll take Johnny to school and will pick him up after my last class this afternoon."

After a few seconds, his only response was, "And dinner?"

"I'll take care of it."

*Just like always.*

---

I entered the Life Drawing classroom, filled with excitement of the unknown. It was an expansive room full of easels placed around a small, elevated, circular stage in the center of the room. The air smelled of paint and solvents. Professor Don Murray moved around the room, distributing supplies to each station. I was the first student to arrive.

"Good morning" he greeted me. "Please come on in and find an easel."

"Sure, I can do that." A nervous laugh escaped my pursed lips. I tried relaxing, with little success.

The remaining students filed in.

"Welcome, ladies and gentlemen. I already know some of you from other classes… hi, Joanne, Almina… ah, and Thomasa. Just to be certain you boarded the right plane today, this is Life Drawing, and I'm Don Murray. We wouldn't want you ending up here when you intended to study Nietzsche or Heidegger's Principle."

We laughed, and he continued with the rules of the road for his class before telling us, "You are all prodigies, unique among all other prodigies. In here you'll learn only the techniques of sketching. Your talent, combined with these techniques, will make it possible for you to succeed. To get a sense of where each of you are with your art, we'll do a two-minute drawing using a live model. This is Mr. Hashi."

I looked past my easel and watched Mr. Hashi proudly walk into position on the stage. There, in all his naked glory, stood a short, slightly pudgy, Japanese version of Michelangelo's David. I quickly shifted my easel to block my view and listened to the professor's instructions.

"Time to use your talents. Is everyone ready?" There was general affirmation from the class. "Draw, people, draw! You have two minutes from… now." He pressed the button on his timer.

I quickly peeked around my easel, ducked back, and began drawing. The sight of a completely naked man standing nonchalantly in front of me unnerved me. With each quick look, I gained enough visual information to draw a portion of Mr. Hashi. I assiduously avoided looking at or drawing his mid-frontal parts.

"Julie, what are you doing?" Professor Murray asked, leaning over my shoulder.

"Umm, uh," I stammered.

"First time drawing a nude?"

"Uh-huh." My eyes remained diverted from our model.

The professor moved my easel, giving me a full view of Mr. Hashi. I waited for the professor to wander off in search of another student to help before I quietly shifted the easel once again, allowing it to act as a shield between me and my embarrassment. I peeked around it again and began sketching Mr. Hashi's right arm and shoulder. Suddenly, my easel appeared to move on its own. The professor had sneaked up behind it and

forcefully turned it, again giving me a full view of our model's …
everything.

Professor Murray stepped onto the stage with our drawing
subject and announced to the class, "I need your attention
please." He put the timer on hold. "I realize, for some of you,
this is the first time you've sketched a nude. In order to know
what you are sketching, you must be able to *see* what you're
sketching. Stop using your easels to shield yourself from your
subject. You are effectively distancing yourself from your art.
Never put barriers between you and what you're drawing, physical or emotional. It will diminish the quality of your work."

The entire class laughed. None of these first-year students
were comfortable in the presence of a nude model. I felt a part
of something—a group of people with common goals and
dreams of a future collectively defusing our embarrassment
with laughter. It was a simple thing, but I rarely felt this kinship
with others.

My routine uniformly consisted of waking at 5 a.m. to get
ready for the day, a day that consisted of doing laundry, singing
the kids awake, dressing them for school and daycare, fixing
breakfast, dropping off the kids at school and daycare, attend-
ing classes most of the day, working a part-time job, picking up
the kids, cleaning house, fixing dinner, singing the kids to sleep,
and studying into the night. Four hours of sleep was a luxury.

Driving to school one Friday during the second year at
WSU, I heard about the National Multiple Sclerosis Society's

annual poster contest on the car radio. Entries were due by noon that day. The morning had been filled to capacity, and I was depressed by the knowledge that I would repeat these days crammed with responsibilities again and again until I graduated. There wasn't time to enter this contest. However, approaching my Graphic Design lecture classroom, inspiration kicked in. Ignoring the speaker, I created a poster of swirling leaves with a bicyclist riding through them, using gouache paint on paper. After class I bought a mat and delivered the painting to the Multiple Sclerosis Society offices at 11:30.

*Whew, where did the motivation for that come from?*

The Society notified me the following Monday that, out of 3,500 entries, my painting was chosen for their poster. I was stunned to win such a prestigious award, having spent so little time on it. Representatives from the foundation presented the award to me during a televised press conference. I felt as proud of this honor as I was of my children. The prizes were a $500 gift card and $500 cash. To my surprise, John was proud of my accomplishment. I looked forward to doing something special for him. He wanted new cowboy boots. I gave him the gift card. He spent the entire amount on his boots. I was disappointed but not surprised. I put the cash in the bank to boost our dwindling money reserves.

The snakeskin boots cheered him up for a short time, but nothing else I did made him happy. He continued to drink heavily, smoke pot, and denigrated everything I did, whether it was schoolwork, cooking, decorating for Christmas, cleaning, or taking care of Johnny and Jessica. He aimed the bulk of his dissatisfaction at me and tried hard to be a good father to

Johnny and Jessica. I knew his growing anger resulted from the changes taking place in me. I was stronger and saw through his weaknesses. I remained firm in my determination to make our marriage work but with little idea how to do it. I kept my eye on the future and held onto my belief that life after graduation would be good.

As much as my drawing, painting, and art history classes enhanced my life, Women's Studies opened my eyes to the world outside the life I had lived during childhood and was living in my marriage. It provided me a perspective of self-worth I had never imagined.

As I read the trials of women from earliest history through the Witches Hammer to the suffragettes and up to the present, I recognized I wasn't alone. My quest to prove I was more than a daughter, wife, mother, cleaner of homes, cooker of meals, and a scapegoat for someone else's shortcomings made me part of a sisterhood of billions of women seeking the same thing. At times I was angry with myself for relenting to the abuse and disdain, for believing I was worthless, but my resolve was stronger than ever to graduate and succeed through art, to never again feel useless.

Prominent among the life lessons was Dr. Ed Harris's "Wilderness Workshop," aimed at getting back to self through nature. Surviving a wilderness experience in Yellowstone Park for two weeks during Dr. Harris's field trip engendered a new sense of power in me. Alone in the park, I sat on the edge of a cliff, wearing a cow bell—worn to deter bears and cougars. The air smelled of pine and cedar and was filled with clarity for the senses, the sky a cerulean blue. Breathing deeply, I replaced the stale air I had brought from home with this wonderful, fresh air as I sketched scenes of waterfalls, rocks, trees, and wildlife. The problems of my world fell away like molted feathers, leaving me with an inner strength and purity of thought. In that moment I knew how to ensure my family's future.

Our bus was late returning to Wichita from Yellowstone. It was dark when I arrived home. The banner on the garage door read "WELCOME HOME, MOMMY" and there were roses in a vase on the kitchen table, the house was clean, and the children had been bathed and were playing in the bedroom. With tears in my eyes, I smiled and held the children close.

"I missed you a whole lot, Mom," Johnny said, returning my hugs.

"Mommy, why are you crying? Are you sad?" Jessica traced a finger down my cheek, catching a tear.

"I'm just so happy to be home. I missed you both more than I could ever imagine. I love you so much."

"I love you too," they said in unison, and Johnny added, "Dad's asleep, and we were being real quiet."

John was half asleep in his recliner and smelled of liquor. He didn't wake when I went to him. My anger with him, long stuffed into a place where it couldn't be expressed, exploded inside me.

*No more. I won't come home to you being dead drunk again.*

*How many times did this happen in my two-week absence? How many times did you leave our kids unattended?*

He was in no condition to comprehend what I had to say. I waited until the children were in bed and he stirred from his stupor.

"John?" I put a cup of coffee in front of him.

He ignored it and me.

"JOHN!"

He raised his head, startled, and glared at me. "Welcome home," he mumbled.

"You need to listen. I want you to get help for your drug and drinking issues."

"I don't have issues. You have a problem. I'm fine with it."

"You know what? You're right. I do have problems with your drinking, using drugs, not working, having no respect for me, and being dead drunk when you're supposed to be taking care of the kids. You're an alcoholic, and I won't live with it anymore. You have to leave."

He laughed. "Yeah? You and what army's gonna throw me out?"

"I'll call the police if you give me any problems with this, but you have to leave. If you get help and quit drinking and using drugs, you can come back, and we'll be the family I always hoped for."

He snorted what I thought was another laugh. I looked again. He was crying. He must have realized he wasn't only leaving me and this wreck of a marriage, he was leaving his children.

I hoped his love for them would inspire him to get help.

He leaned back in his recliner. After intimidating me for

years, he seemed broken, more sad than angry at my ultimatum.

"You have until morning to pack your stuff and leave. Let me know when you get help and tell me how it's going. We'll talk again when you're sober for good."

I locked myself in the children's bedroom with Johnny and Jessica and waited. Around midnight I heard him yelling and thrashing around in the kitchen. Not knowing what he might do, I stayed quiet. A glass broke against a wall. Then I heard him pack his belongings and load them into his truck. He cursed my name as he left the final time, slamming the front door hard enough to wake Jessica. He started the truck and drove away. I assumed he left without confronting me because he shared my misery of our marriage.

I learned the next day that he moved in with his buddy, Fogey, and arrived with another woman in tow.

Between 30-50 years of age,
the first typical signs of
aging appear in the features
of almost all people.
The development of these
signs depend on the
physical type,
the way of life
and health.

Healthy people usually
maintain their fresh
appearance longer.
Others, such as the BTK,
who suffer from  mental
or physical illmess
have abnormally
colored complexions,
and show age sooner
then most.

The most characteristic sign
of middle age, peculiar
to all persons, is the
development of the
skull bones, which
emphasize the
prominences and
cavities of the
facial relief.

In some
people, the
adipose cells
develop excessively,
causing fatness of the
face, in other people,  the
adipose cells become
exhausted, causing a general
shrinking and thinning
of the face.

It is very difficult to determine
exactly the changes which
take place in the human
face during various perods
of life.  Often a man over
thirty years, who's had
many trials, appears
much older than his age.

While in youth, character is
being formed, and in old age
its development is lessening,
in middle age it appears it
is maximum development.
The facial muscles reach their
maximum expressiveness,
owing to the extreme
development of the
physical and psychical
peculiarities.

# Chapter 15

# Aging a Serial Killer

His eyes were the greatest challenge. I had imagined BTK's featureless face for so long in my nightmares that I couldn't perceive his eyes. The thought of sketching them filled me with horror. But I needed to crawl behind them in order to reflect their depravity, their selfish, their narcissistic thirst for killing.

The glacial descriptions of the murders in the cold case files helped me understand the BTK killer's mode of killing. My imagination imbued me with his victims' terror. The next step was to study the flip-chart composites of BTK that had been prepared from eyewitness reports. I used them to decide what the BTK strangler had looked like at age 26, my baseline for aging him.

In 1991, flip charts were commonly used to build composite images of suspects. They contained pages showing common eye shapes, nose configurations, mustaches, facial outlines, and hair color and styles. As the witness described a culprit, the police sketch artist flipped through specific aspects on the charts until the witness selected the one closest to his or her memory. The method had many shortcomings. It was not possible to capture emotion, age, or dimension in flip-chart drawings.

Eyewitnesses in the BTK cases ranged from those who survived an attack to those who believed they saw him driving a victim's car or noticed him as a stranger walking through a victim's neighborhood.

All of the witnesses experienced severe trauma; some required hypnosis to recall the killer's face. For a few witnesses, recall was impossible, even under hypnosis. For example, a fireman had been standing outside a phone booth, waiting to make a call, while BTK, in the phone booth, reported the murder of Nancy Fox. Police traced the fireman's call back to the person he telephoned, which eventually led them to him. When he learned that the man talking on the phone in front of him had been BTK, he was so shocked and frightened that he couldn't recall anything about the man's face.

Of the descriptions, four were good enough to produce flip-chart drawings, but none resembled any of the others. While reviewing the four, blended drawings, I noticed some nuanced similarities, beginning with facial shape and eyes. I selected the one containing the largest number of connections to the others. This sketch had a flat appearance lacking in expression and character, reflecting the one-dimensional shortcoming of flip-chart composites. I used it for the age 26 drawing because it gave me the basis for his head shape, eyes, chin, and nose. The goal was to produce drawings of BTK at age 46 or 47 that reflected his demeanor, with and without a moustache, with a receding hairline or a full head of hair, and with and without a double chin.

I used the concepts learned from my life drawing classes and studies of the masters to age him. Working at home or at the WSU library helped me concentrate. The room at the detectives squad was too noisy and distracting.

I postulated that BTK was healthy, based on general eyewitness reports. As an able-bodied person, he would show the signs of aging slower than a drug addict, an alcoholic, someone suffering from depression, or anyone who leads an unhealthy lifestyle. I assumed he led a "normal" personal life, and from the investigators and the FBI, I learned killing gave him pleasure.

However, the stress from his constant fear of capture, and the emotional weight of balancing his everyday life with his crimes, would show in his face as he aged. At 46 or 47, he would look older than a average, well-adjusted man.

Toward middle age, the prominences and cavities of his facial relief would be more pronounced, and his facial bones and nose would widen. In some people, adipose (fat) cells develop, causing further broadening of the face, nose, and chin. In other people, fat cells deplete, causing a general shrinking and thinning of the face. Based on BTK's assumed health, I drew his face somewhat enlarged with fat cells at 47 and included bags under his eyes and the beginning of jowls. All of these are definitive marks of a man at the mid-point of his life.

The dread of crawling through his dark soul to understand him made my hands shake as I worked to capture his eyes in middle age. Using the basic shape from the earlier composite, I sketched the shape of his 47-year-old eyes based on changes in the shape of the skull as it ages.

Having completed the substructure of the eyes, I tried to get inside this man's mind. What would the eyes of a man who could kill children see? Would the windows to his soul be dark holes, devoid of expression, or like a wild animal in search of  blood sport? I needed to picture how those eyes would appear at rest, when he was angry, when he concentrated, under the stress of potential capture, and when he killed. Imagining how they looked with each emotion, I visualized the distinctive wrinkles and bags that would have accumulated over time.

Next, I shone the limelight on his mouth. It's the second part of a person's face that is most vulnerable to the ravages of emotion. His lips had been fairly full at 26 but would pucker over time. The wrinkles around his mouth would reflect repeated pursing as he planned and committed the murders. It was important that I match the power of the accumulated stress of his mouth with that of his eyes.

Trawling inside the mind of a serial killer to gain insights for a drawing sapped my strength, intensified my nightmares, and caused me to doubt the existence of a merciful God.

———

I delivered the completed drawings to Ken Landwehr in August 1991. The day was suffocating and had Kansas summer written all over it. It cycled between searing heat and searing heat with a strong dry wind. The weather and the completion of the sketches left me feeling desiccated.

The detectives squad buzzed with activity as I walked in.

"Hi, Julie, if you're here for more files, you'll need to wait. We're in the middle of something here." Ken Landwehr breezed by me in the too-cold room.

"Don't need files today. I finished the drawings."

He stopped. He was busy and this interruption brought a frown to his brow. "Okay, let's take a look."

"Landwehr! We're waiting over here," someone bellowed over the noise.

"On my way, captain." I tried to hand him the drawings but he waved them away, saying, "Keep them and wait for me, if you can. I really have to go." He turned and hurried away, leaving me standing in the middle of controlled chaos.

*Okay, I'll wait.*

I had been watching the activity around me for only a few moments when Ken returned and motioned to me to follow him. "Let's go in here." He led me into a familiar room. "When I told the captain you had the sketches of BTK ready, he asked me why I was making you wait." He smiled and opened the door.

*My research room.*

The air chilled everything in it, including me.

*Is their air conditioner set on Stun?*

"There are six sketches in the brochure. I researched how the human face changes over the years and assumed BTK's face would reflect the emotional weight of his crimes." I handed Ken the brochure with a mixture of pride and anxiety.

"Let's see what you brought us." His face reflected surprise. "Very nice! The eyes, they're great. The emotional turmoil he must feel is there. Great job, Julie."

I didn't realize I had been holding my breath. A deep inhale and I breathed again.

"Can we keep these for a while?"

"I need to submit the brochure to the professor for my final grade next week, but you can have them until then. I'll only need the pamphlet for about a week. I'll give them back to you after I get my grade."

"You'll be rewarded for this work one day, Julie. You may be responsible for helping us find BTK. Once we capture him—and we *will* capture him—we'll be able to use your name and pay you for the sketches. Until then we'll keep your association with them in the strictest confidence."

"Okay, then, I'll let you get back to work. I'll come by and pick them up next week."

"Thanks again. Really good work."

We shook hands and I left, returning to my other life, which was indelibly changed by the process of drawing the BTK.

During the four months after I delivered the drawings, they had a regular spot on Wichita television news programs that warned everyone of the unidentified serial killer who was still at large. "If you know or see someone who resembles these pictures, police ask that call the number on your screen. This man is a dangerous serial killer."

## Chapter 16

# Single Mom, Three Kids

A rare, mild day in August greeted us. Trees were parched from several days of temperatures exceeding 100 degrees, and their leaves crackled in the light breeze. Johnny and Jessica climbed the jungle gym at Sedgwick County Park. Jessica squealed as she raced down the slide. We had brought a picnic lunch in a cooler for an all-too-infrequent day in the park together. I was the sole breadwinner and worked two jobs at times to keep us afloat. John had little contact with us. Now living with his parents, he rarely worked and continued to struggle with his addiction to drugs and alcohol.

"Mommy, watch me," Johnny yelled.

*If I had a nickel for every time I heard of that sentence.*

I smiled. "I'm watching. I've never seen anybody swing that high!"

Jessica ran to me, throwing her little arms around my legs and squeezing hard. It was a toddler's reassurance hug. I bent down to reciprocate. Standing up, I saw a man approaching the swingset where Johnny was playing. The other children on the playground were with their moms. This man was out of place. My stomach clutched in a knot of fear. I scooped Jessica into my arms and ran toward the swings. "HEY!" I shouted at the man. He looked up, startled, then stooped and picked up the soccer ball lying in the path of Johnny's swing.

*Okay, Julie, breathe. This is not BTK.*

"Sorry, I thought you were running into the path of my son's swing." I lied, trying to diffuse the offense.

"No problem." He waved and handed the ball to his approaching son.

*I see danger everywhere since I turned over my sketches to the police. At least now my imagined stalkers have faces.*

But the fear was real. I jumped at shadows and now at dads chasing soccer balls. I wondered if I would ever be able to enjoy a life without the anxiety of BTK and the panic I experienced daily.

<hr>

When Ken Landwehr returned the original sketches to me, he reinforced his assurance that my name wouldn't be associated with the age-progression drawings until BTK's capture. I was still known only as "The Sketcher." It should have helped, but the FBI profiled that BTK could be in law enforcement. There were so many people involved with the task force, and in my mind it could be one of them. No one knew the identity of this monster. The only person I fully trusted was Ken. My drawings were almost daily reminders on television news, always shown along with the film of the murdered Otero family being carried from their home in body bags.

I prayed every day that someone would recognize BKT from the drawings and turn in their uncle or husband or the guy next door, and this ceaseless nightmare would end. The dreams of being suffocated and my suspicion of men who resembled my sketches would also end. My prayers were not answered.

<hr>

For almost a year after we separated, John and I kept in touch during his visits with Johnny and Jessica. He remained firm about not getting help, and his contempt for me grew. When he ridiculed me in front of the children, I told him if he ever did it again, he wouldn't see the kids. Our children should never be put in the position to choose between their mom and dad, and when he degraded me in front of them, he forced them to make a choice. He continued to demean me in their presence.

As graduation approached in May 1992, John's attitude improved. He began courting me again. He called, excited to let me know he had a job with a survey company and wanted me to give him a second chance. I realized how difficult working was for John. The fall from the oil derrick years before had left him in almost constant pain. He seemed sincere and determined to stay sober, but without professional help, I didn't have much confidence. We saw each other a few times to test the waters.

"Listen, Julie, I want to throw a graduation party for you." John's call surprised me.

"Can you afford that? I mean, you just started working again?" I caught myself before going on, certain he would be offended. I was wrong.

"Yeah. I moved into an apartment, and they have a party room." He continued, "I reserved it so I could make sure it was ours to use. They don't charge for us to use it." He was earnest and trying hard to do this right.

"Okay, besides my parents and your parents, can we invite our brothers?" My brothers were as wild as March hares, but they wanted to come to my graduation.

"Sure, and some friends."

It was settled; everyone who came to the graduation ceremony, plus some friends, would attend. John planning the party for me was unsettling. Getting to know each other again after almost a year of separation was a big enough step. I didn't want to feel obligated to him, but I felt guilty turning him down.

My high spirits on graduation day obliterated all doubt about the party. It was a time to celebrate this accomplishment, and we did, with everyone on their best behavior.

I let John back into our lives. It was short lived. He began drinking again, and I found drug paraphernalia in the house. I sent him away. He couldn't stay sober and off drugs without help, and he was too stubborn to seek help. I refused to allow the children to be subjected to a drunken, drug-addicted dad, and I wouldn't live with it any longer. After 13 years, our marriage was over.

A month later, I discovered I was pregnant.

---

John's attitude toward me deteriorated after we separated for the second time. He filed for divorce, lost his job again, refused to recognize the baby I carried as his child, and couldn't contribute financially. An annulment from the church was granted within weeks of our final breakup.

Without his help, we weren't able to stay in the house we had bought together. The three and a half of us moved into an inexpensive duplex in West Wichita. My new ambition was to buy a home for us.

During fall of 1992, as my body began showing signs of

pregnancy, I was just hired as an associate professor, teaching communication at WSU, and as an intern graphic designer at KAKE-TV, Channel 10. I saved every penny possible toward the down payment on a house.

By May 17, 1993, when I went into labor, living alone again with my fears of BTK was routine. I went to bizarre limits to ensure our safety. When the nurses rolled my gurney into the operating room for a C-section, I wouldn't let the surgical team continue with the delivery until they removed their scrub masks so I could see their faces. No one asked me for an explanation. They politely removed their surgical masks. I looked at each face and nodded. They replaced their masks and delivered my charming little Jackie.

My girlfriend tried to contact John, who had ignored the message that I was in labor with our third child. Jacqueline Thimmesch came into our lives without her father in attendance. She was a tie with Jessica's sweetness of temperament and beauty. She captured our hearts. Her dad, however, refused to see her. He turned down all opportunities to be a part of this beautiful child's life. I never forgave him.

John tried to maintain his relationship with Johnny and Jessica, but over time he drifted away from all of us.

Now a single mother of three with no resources, I learned to rely on my own efforts. It was easy to become accustomed to living without the daily specter of John's addictions, but the nightmares and occasional imaginary sightings of BTK remained commonplace. Our lives were better in some respects, but we continued to struggle financially. My focus remained on providing a happy home for my children, one without the abuse

I had experienced as a child. I rejected any offers my parents made to see the kids. I would never allow them to influence Johnny, Jessica, or Jackie or take the chance that their anger over some misbehavior would turn to physical violence. John's parents were my children's grandparents.

However, when Jackie was four months old, my relationship with my parents changed dramatically. My sweet Jackie was one of three babies who contracted pertussis from DPT shots they received from Wichita Clinic. Jackie was the only one to survive. She was in intensive care at Wesley Hospital for a month and lost four pounds. I had a new job and couldn't spend the amount of time with her that she deserved. When Mom and Dad found out that John refused to recognize her as his child, they pitched in and took turns staying at the hospital, rocking her and caring for her when I couldn't be there. They adored new babies. It was the first time in my life that I saw sparks of humanity in my parents. I puzzled at what happened to that love as their babies grew. Was it buried under piles of need to keep order in a house with eight children?

John ordered his mother not to see Jackie during this time. Not helping with the care of her granddaughter was more than she could bear. When Joann rounded the corner of the pediatric intensive care unit, she was devastated by the severity of Jackie's condition. She came back every day, holding and rocking Jackie as she cried for missing out on the opportunity to help her grandbaby sooner. Jackie became the love of Joann's life, and Joann was, forever after, my helpmate with the children.

The phone rang, an unwelcome interruption on a Saturday morning. It was the mother of Jessica's friend Mary. She planned a birthday party for Mary and invited Jessica to spend the night with them.

I discovered that the little girl's home was a health hazard, with overflowing toilets and animal feces on the floor while Mary's baby sister sat nearby, eating off that floor. Jessica did not spend the night, but I saw potential in the house and knew I could make a home out of it.

Mary's family planned to move to Kansas City and was vacating the rented house. I contacted the owners, who accepted my offer to buy and provided financing. I bought it with $65.05 down payment. Having seen her friend's house when it was filthy and pest ridden, six-year-old Jessica cried when I told her it would be our new home.

"When we move into the house, it won't look anything like it did when you saw it, baby. I promise."

She remained skeptical.

With $2,000 savings, I hired a plumber to replace fixtures. I bought paint and cleaning materials, including muriatic acid to clean the toilets. Friends and I—dressed in our finest hazmat gear, dust masks, and rubber gloves—pulled up carpet, refinished the wood flooring we uncovered, cleaned the house, and painted the walls and decorated them with my sketches. My children and I had a home, and I bought it with no one's help.

When we moved into our house in 1994, Johnny was twelve, Jessica seven, and Jackie was nearly two.

While John and I were married, John spent more time with our children than I did. He knew how to play with them. They cherished their dad and he adored them. Between work and school, there had been few occasions for me to play with them. Now, without school on my schedule, I had more time available to spend with them. That's when I discovered I didn't know how to clown around with my children.

I don't remember playing as a child. I had always been on point, watching for my parents' reactions to everything I did. My brothers and I were always on the edge of fear or immersed in it. Our parents controlled us with fear. Drawing and singing were my private pastimes in childhood, and the only ways I knew to entertain my children.

---

"Sing it again, Mommy," Jessica called to me from the back-seat of our car. "Sing it again."

She meant the song "Susie Q," the one my grandpa sang to me when we fished together. Her favorite phrase was, "I love you, Susie Q."

"Let's try another song," I coaxed

"No, Mommy, no. Sing "Susie Q," pleeeeese?" And we sang it again.

Other times we competed to see who could reach the highest notes singing the Doobie Brothers or Black Water arrangements. I sang the children to sleep and made up nonsense songs to wake them in the mornings. Some became requested favorites.

Johnny, Jessica, and Jackie were my favorite company. I loved talking to them, watching them play softball, riding their bikes in the park. Each day with them was an opportunity to break the cycle of mistreatment with kindness to this new generation. I wouldn't allow abuse to be a part of their lives, and I would heal hand in hand with their happiness. They have always been the best of my life.

The four of us were a family. We laughed and cried, argued and made up, and lived every day with the love and respect that had been missing from my childhood family and my life with John. I was surprised how easy it was to live harmoniously.

And then I started dating Kyle.

Chapter 17

# A New Beginning

Johnny won at Clue and Jessica was not happy about losing. The game was age appropriate for Johnny but too advanced for five-year-old Jessica. My help irritated her. She wanted to win it on her own, but Johnny had the advantage and could see through the mysteries to the solutions.

"I don't like this game," my darling daughter announced. "I want to play Hungry Hippo," the game she won twice earlier that evening. It was also the game her brother let her win most of the time. He was unerringly kind to his sister, but it was time for the challenge of Clue and for Johnny to win a few games.

"How about playing Mouse Trap next?" was my peace offering.

"Yeah, that'd be great, huh, Jess?" Johnny encouraged.

Jessica scurried away to find the game.

The phone rang. "I'll get that. You kids set up the game." With its Rube Goldberg contraption of a game board, setting up Mouse Trap was almost as much fun as playing the game.

"How are you doing these days, Julie?" It was Kyle Hall.

"We're good here."

Kyle lived near our house in Orchard Park. A neighbor had introduced us after John and I divorced. Kyle had stayed in touch with us after we moved from the house John and I bought. I kept him at arm's length. I wasn't ready to be involved in another relationship. My close associations with men had not engendered trust.

"What do you want, Kyle?"

Ignoring my abruptness, he soldiered on. "I thought you and the kids would like to go to the zoo this weekend. The weather is supposed to be good. We'll take a picnic lunch."

"I have a lot of work to catch up on here at the house."

"Aw, come on, it'll be fun. Kids love the zoo, and you like whatever makes your kids happy, right?" He was persistent.

One thing in Kyle's favor, he always included the kids in his plans. He appeared to love children and was generous with mine. He had a stable job and a nice house, was a calm person, and seemed reliable.

*May be worth taking a chance here.*

"You still there, Julie?"

"Uh, yeah. You know, the zoo sounds like a good time. Thanks."

"We'll go early, around ten. I'll pick you up at nine thirty."

*He's telling me what we're going to do, not asking me. Maybe he's just decisive. Settle yourself.*

But the red flag gave me a cautionary moment.

"We'll be ready. 'Bye now."

The zoo trip was a tremendous success. Johnny's favorites were the lions and the giant python. Jessica fell head over heels for the river otters. Jackie giggled when I showed her the giraffes and elephants.

I enjoyed the easy camaraderie with Kyle. He was relaxed with the kids most of the time. He showed a flash of anger at one point when Jessica ran ahead of us. He yelled at her to come back "Now!" and my sensors went off again. Jessica was surprised that he was angry with her, but she came back and seemed unaffected by his outburst. Otherwise, he wasn't stressed by my kids acting like kids. I scrutinized him every second, and he came through looking pretty good.

*Cautionary red flags notwithstanding, this guy's worth a second look.*

A second look became a third, a fourth, and before I knew it, I had collected a mountain of red flags that I rationalized away. When he asked me to marry him, I ran through the plus and minus columns in my head. The fact that he had a stable job and was generous trumped the entire list of control and anger issues I witnessed while we dated. I was worn out from working two jobs to barely make ends meet and from doing the work of two parents. Kyle loved my kids and his son from a previous marriage, Shane, and he offered us financial security for what seemed a small price: managing his anger for him.

My last terrifying dream about BTK had been the night before we went to the zoo.

⸺⸺⸺

Doubts continued to nag at me and I ignored them. A couple of weeks before my birthday in 1997, and a day after Kyle lost his temper and yelled at me in front of the children, he called me after work. He was exuberant.

"Guess what I did today?"

"I give up. What did you do today?" I joked.

"I bought plane tickets to Boston and rented a bungalow on the beach in Cape Cod for your birthday. One of my favorite aunts lives in the Boston area, too, and you can meet her. You know, meet more of my family."

"That sounds fabulous. When?"

"In two weeks. We'll fly away back East just like you told me you always wanted to do."

"I'll have to check and see if I can get the time off at work."

*I wish you had let me know before making the reservations*

I believed it was a spur-of-the moment act of contrition for having lost his temper. I pushed it aside, but it remained a thought. No one had offered to take me on a trip before. I believed mentioning it out loud would look like I didn't appreciate his gesture, but it added another red flag to the pile.

The trip was my dream come true. We bicycled around the island, ate picnic lunches on the beach, laughed when we were soaked by the rain, and lived the tourist life to the hilt. It was romantic and smoothed the ragged edges that were beginning to appear in our relationship, raw places caused by Kyle's anger and efforts to control me. I returned from Massachusetts with a renewed confidence that our marriage had a chance.

# Chapter 18

# Rudy

"I'm leaving now; I have to watch those builders like a hawk. I'll call when I think of something for us to do today." Kyle checked the progress daily on the house we were building.

It was a Saturday morning two weeks before Kyle's and my wedding, and the kids and I were taking our time getting ready for the day. We enjoyed the leisure of no softball practice or ball games, no place to be but home. Four-year-old Jackie was absorbed by a Saturday morning cartoon, oblivious to her siblings squabbling nearby. Johnny sat on the couch, playing Donkey Kong, while Jessica kibitzed over his shoulder, annoying him. It's what little sisters do with their older brothers.

"Qui-i-i-it! Mo-o-o-om, Jess won't leave me alone."

"She doesn't mean any harm."

"Yeah, but she's buggin' me."

"Jessica, find something else to do and stop bugging your brother."

"Ow. Mo-o-om, Johnny smacked me."

"Uhn-n-n-n-N. Who wants to spend some quality time in their bedroom without Donkey Kong or TV?"

The bugging and smacking stopped.

When the phone rang, interrupting the family dynamics, I expected it to be Kyle with a plan for the day. I would have to tell him this was a day for no plans.

"Is this Julie Riedel?" a man on the other end of the line asked.

"It is, but the last name is Thimmesch now, and if you're selling something, I can't afford it, no matter how cheap it is."

The man laughed. "I'm Father Patrick York from Our Lady

of Lourdes parish in Pittsburg, Kansas."

"Yes, Father York, I think we met a few years ago." I was puzzled, baffled about why a man I had chatted with at a retreat five years before would call me.

"I found a contact number for you through St. Francis of Assisi parish, which is where we met as I recall." He hesitated. "I have someone here who wants to meet you."

"Oh—" In that instant, I knew who it was. Tears came to my eyes before Father York could tell me.

"This young man's name is Rudy Draper. He traced the records of his birth to you and would like to meet you. I'm his intermediary."

"He's the baby … the baby I gave up … gave up for adoption in 1977. I was seventeen years old. When you said, 'There is someone here who wants to meet you,' I knew. I *knew*." I had to catch my breath. "Is everything okay with him?"

"Oh, yes, he's healthy and happy … one of the greatest kids I've ever met."

"When … when can I meet him? I mean, he does want to meet me, right?"

*This must be a dream and I'm going to wake up any minute.*

"He definitely wants to meet you. I can drive him to Wichita this weekend if that works for you."

"Yes, that's perfect. Thank you *so* much. My address is Eight Forty-four Caddy in Wichita. Do you need directions to find us?"

"Directions aren't needed, I know Wichita pretty well. We can be there around ten on Saturday morning. Rudy is over-the-moon happy at the prospect of meeting you, and I'm looking forward to seeing you again."

"Thank you, thank you, Father. Have a safe trip." My stomach clutched at the prospect of telling the kids about their half-brother and revealing the newest member of our family to Kyle.

I talked with Kyle while we sat outside watching the steaks cook on the grill. He wasn't concerned about Rudy being the result of my carnal knowledge outside of marriage.

"I just don't think it's a good idea to make him of part of our family."

"Because?" I was mystified by his position on this.

"I had a friend down in Texas who did that, and it was a disaster. The kid was a screw-up and all he ever wanted was money."

*That's them, not us. How can you be so short-sighted?*

"Father York says he's a good kid … one of the best kids he knows."

"Still not a good idea. I'm telling you, don't do it."

*Your opinion doesn't matter in this. It's my life too.*

"I know this is going to be difficult for you to accept, but I *am* going to meet Rudy, and if Johnny, Jessica, and Jackie like him, I'm gonna make him a part of our lives. He *is* and always has been a part of me. Yeah, meeting him will be hard on all of us, but he's a kid finding his way. He deserves to meet us. When he comes here, if you can be kind to him and welcome him, you can stay for the meeting. If you can't do that, then please, just don't be here."

"Fine by me. I don't want to have anything to do with him. I'm telling you, you'll be sorry you let some stranger into your life like this."

*Yeah, well, you were a stranger to me once too, and I let you into my life. Should I be sorry about that?*

The conversation was short and clear, but standing up for myself worked this time.

I planned a special meal for Johnny, Jessica, and Jackie, plying them with fried chicken, mashed potatoes, and gravy, their favorites. Gathering the kids for a sit-down dinner was like corralling smoke. With so many sports practices, homework, and friends, it was a challenge, but the day before Rudy and I were to meet, their schedules worked for us to talk. Kyle spent the evening at the new house, making certain it was perfect for our family to move into before the wedding.

Conversation was chaotic at first with everyone trying to talk at once.

"Hello, the table! I have something important to tell you."

Jessica jabbered on.

"Hey, Jess, BE QUIET. Mom has something to tell us." Johnny to the rescue.

Jessica stopped talking.

"I want you to know about what's happening tomorrow."

All eyes were on me.

"A boy named Rudy is coming to see us. He's nineteen years old, and he's your half-brother." With my kids, the easiest way to talk about something difficult is to just *say* it and deal with the outcome. My successes with John and Kyle were more limited using that approach.

Jackie was too little to comprehend but remained still, copying her brother and sister.

I continued. "I had Rudy when I was seventeen years old. I was too young to be a good mom."

"But you're always a good mom." Johnny, seeing the hurt building in my eyes, reassured me.

"Thanks, Johnny. Come to think of it, I was only a year older than you are. Anyway, another mom and dad adopted Rudy and took care of him. Now he wants to meet us." I could feel my face reddening and tears welling. "He'll be here tomorrow morning."

"So, it's like we have this grownup brother?" Johnny offered. "Cool. Do we get to meet him too?"

I nodded acknowledgement. "Yes and yes."

"I want to meet him too, Mom." Jessica's wrapped her arms around me.

"Well, except for Jackie, I guess that makes it unanimous." I laughed.

Johnny smiled. "Yeah, but Jackie likes everybody, don't you, Jackie?"

She nodded her head. "Yeah. Me too, Mommy."

As I shed tears of gratitude for the three best children in the world, we had one of the most memorable group hugs in our family's history.

———

I started Saturday with confession at St. Francis Assisi and a prayer for strength and guidance that our meeting with Rudy would bring us joy and comfort.

It was a typical Kansas summer day: cloudless, hot in the morning, hotter at noon, and sweltering by evening. By the time Father York pulled into my driveway at 10 a.m., it was nearing 100 degrees, and the driveway forced heat through the soles of our sandals. The air was redolent with the smell of hot asphalt.

Waiting on the driveway for our guest to arrive, Johnny asked, "Why isn't Kyle here to meet Rudy too?"

"He'll meet Rudy in his own time. He isn't ready to accept anyone else into our family right now."

A car pulled into the driveway. I caught the first sight of my oldest son. Memories of his birth and not being allowed to hold him haunted me, and now he was a sandy-haired 19-year-old unfolding his six foot muscular frame from Father York's car.

The kids flanked me as though they were there to catch me if I fainted.

"Hello, Julie. It's good to see you again." Father York turned to the handsome young man beside him "Rudy Draper, this is Julie Thimmesch, your birth mother, and if you don't mind me saying it, the resemblance between the two of you is remarkable."

"I've waited all my life to meet you," Rudy began.

Tears overflowed to my cheeks.

"Is it okay if I call you Mom?"

"Oh my God, yes, YES!" I threw my arms around him and held him for the first time.

"And who are these guys?" Rudy asked, looking at his siblings. His eyes glistened with tears.

"I'm not a guy!" Jessica blurted.

Rudy laughed. "Of course you're not."

I introduced him to Johnny, Jessica, Jackie, and Kyle's son, Shane. They were shy at first. Seeing me cry, four-year-old Jackie was concerned that I was sad about this tall stranger coming to see us. I reassured her with a hug. We gravitated to the air-conditioned house. While Father York kept Jackie and Shane occupied, Johnny, Jessica, Rudy, and I talked. The ease of our conversation was like old friends catching up after a long separation.

Talking above the squeals of laughter coming from the other room, Rudy told us about his life, his adoptive parents, Joyce and Barry Draper, his two siblings, and growing up in Pittsburgh, Kansas. Rudy adored his parents. The nuns at Catholic Charities had given him to a family who loved and cared for him, just as I had asked. Joyce and Barry Draper had encouraged Rudy to find his birth parents, leading him to me. He had already located his birth father. To Tom's discredit, he wanted nothing to do with Rudy.

The kids told stories of the sports they played. Rudy had bragging rights, having played football in high school. Johnny was impressed. It was common ground. We laughed at the stories of growing up and the silly things we did. Rudy told us about his girlfriend, Becca. He wanted us to meet her … and, he announced, "I joined the Marines."

Surprised looks all around.

"In a few days, I leave for thirteen weeks of basic training in San Diego. I wanted to meet you before I left." He hesitated and asked, "Is there … um, uh … is there any chance you could come to San Diego when I graduate from basic training? Becca and my parents are coming. You could meet them then."

Accepting Rudy in our lives was not a question, it was the conclusion.

I promised we would be there and told him I was excited he would be finished in time for Kyle's and my wedding in Kansas.

*Maybe it's a good thing Kyle isn't going to San Diego to see Rudy right now.*

With time, I was certain Kyle would change his mind about getting to know Rudy.

Johnny, Becca, and I flew to San Diego, and along with Joyce and Barry Draper, we were Rudy's loud cheering section when he graduated, standing tall in full uniform with his shoulders back. I couldn't stop smiling. After the ceremonies, we met Rudy's drill sergeant.

With his hand on Rudy's shoulder, the sergeant asked if Rudy had told us about his basic training.

I put my arm around Rudy's waist. "Yes, he did."

The sergeant turned a stern gaze on Johnny. "Did he tell you *everything?*"

Johnny didn't answer. He tried to appear smaller than his tall, lanky, 15-year-old self.

Still looking at Johnny, the sergeant narrowed his eyes. "See you in few years, kid. You're *mine!*" He walked away, chuckling to himself.

Johnny's eyes were wide. Rudy nudged him. "The sarge is tough, but he's a good guy."

*A good guy like both of my sons.*

## Chapter 19

# Four and a Half Years

Kyle wanted the best of everything for us. I designed the house plan: one with a bedroom for each child and space for me to set up my easel and paint or sketch. We hired an architect to develop the drawings. It was the house of all our dreams. Kyle hired contractors and had the house built before our wedding. I was overjoyed with the opportunity to give my children a secure life. As our lives improved, my BTK-induced fear of strangers diminished.

Kyle's and my wedding was a small intimate affair on July 26, 1997. We were married in St. Francis of Assisi church, decorated in peach. Johnny, Shane, our parents, my brothers, and Kyle's sisters attended. My two beautiful girls, Jackie and Jessica, were our flower girl and ring bearer. Rudy had just completed basic training in San Diego, and was able to attend the wedding.

We spent our honeymoon in Cancun, Mexico, lounging on the beach, drinking Sangria, and talking about our future: it was bright and secure, painted the colors of a rainbow.

---

The phone rang one morning a few days after we returned from our honeymoon.

"Hello, may I speak with Mrs. Hall?"

"I'm Julie Hall."

"This is Kim Wentworth, I'm a counselor at Charter Hospital."

"What's this about?"

"Human Resources at Boeing mandated a series of

counselling session for your husband, Kyle. Part of the process is a group counseling session with you and Kyle's parents. It's scheduled for eight a.m. on Thursday at Charter Hospital."

"I don't understand. What's this about?"

"Please talk with your husband about the particulars of this case."

"Of course I will, but can't you tell me what's going on?"

"I'm sorry, Mrs. Hall, but I can't. Will you attend the counseling session?"

"Yes, of course. Yes. Will you be there?"

"I will. See you Thursday, ma'am."

I speculated something must have happened at work, his temper may have flared. That evening I confronted Kyle about the appointment.

"It's not a big deal. I have a few drinks at lunch once in a while and was late to work a few times."

"Counseling sessions mandated by your boss *are* a big deal!"

"Let's not get excited about it, okay. You, Mom, and Pops just need to be there to support me, that's all."

Still unaccustomed to challenging him, I didn't demand a more detailed explanation. I knew he drank a little but never to excess. He was always mellow and in a better mood after he had a couple of drinks in the evenings. Mornings were the most difficult time of the day for Kyle. He was angry at the world in the morning, and he had trouble getting to work on time. We had encountered his morning anger issues a few times before we married and several times afterward. As difficult as it was getting three kids ready for school, we quickly learned to stay out of his way early in the day.

Early on the morning of the counselling session, Kyle was in his usual foul mood. I remained quiet during the drive, not wanting to annoy him. I had so many questions to ask but was too fearful of the answers. We arrived at Charter Hospital early. The weather threatened storms and there was a humid heaviness in the air. As we walked across the parking lot, the sky opened, drenching us.

"Didn't you bring a damned umbrella?"

"No. Just run, Kyle, we'll dry off when we get inside."

The rain and no umbrella didn't improve his outlook.

The woman at the information desk directed us to a meeting room. A propped-open door greeted us. A tall, thin woman around 40 sat in a chair pulled slightly out of sync with an arc of chairs where Kyle, his parents, and I would sit.

"Kim?"

"Yes, I'm Kim Wentworth. You're Kyle and Julie Hall?" She gave us a stiff smile.

We acknowledged that we were Kyle and Julie and shook hands.

"Why are there so many chairs?" Kyle asked.

"Kyle, your parents are also joining us today."

Mary and Dean Hall arrived at that moment and introduced themselves to Kim.

"This is called an intervention," Kim began, speaking directly to Kyle. "The people in attendance are the ones closest to you. I'll monitor the conversation to keep everyone on track, and your family will talk with you openly and honestly about your drinking and try to determine why it's hard for you to make it to work on time." Looking at Kyle's parents and me, she continued,

"The round of counseling that Kyle is required to attend was mandated by his employer."

Kyle shifted in his chair and challenged Kim. "So what if I just walk out?"

"Your employer will be informed, and he will take action he deems necessary."

"Which means I'll get fired, right?"

This threat to our security made me nauseous.

"I don't know what he might do, Kyle. The important thing we want to accomplish here is to give you insights into how your problems affect the people closest to you. Then we need to decide what course of action we think will make things better."

I was the only person in the room unprepared to talk about Kyle's "problems." Interventions address problems that interfere with day-to-day lives. Drinking wasn't on my radar as a problem with Kyle, and while he had anger issues, they only occurred in the mornings. His temper didn't come close to the dark rages from my childhood. I didn't know the reason Kyle was a terror in the morning but mellow later in the day. Maybe the few drinks he had late in the day took the edge off his stress.

Kyle's parents talked with him about his responsibility to be on time for work and his antagonism in the mornings. The kids and I had learned early in our relationship with him to avoid disagreeing or doing anything that might anger him in the mornings, but I had no intention of discussing it at this meeting. I already felt responsible for his tantrums. I didn't need a counselor reinforcing my guilt. God, I was screwed up then. I felt comfortable being obligated for his fury but was disturbed discussing it with a counselor.

Kyle finished the mandated sessions and stopped drinking. His bouts of anger in the mornings stretched into afternoons and evenings, becoming worse until we walked on eggs most of the time he was home.

The counseling helped him stop drinking, and he was no longer late to work. However, the core of his problem—his inability to control his temper—became worse. The counselor cured him of using the only thing that calmed his rage. She missed the base issue in her quest to help Kyle get to work on time. I was no help, because I couldn't talk about his morning outrages during our group session for fear of making them worse. The entire effort was doomed to failure from the start.

—————

We settled into our new house, and our family fell into a routine that worked for us most of the time. When Kyle was home, everyone was quiet, respectful, and the kids disappeared into their rooms. When he took out his ire on one of us, Kyle rewarded the object of his anger with a present and an apology afterwards.

By the first spring of the new millennium, I was pregnant with my fifth child. Johnny, Jessica, and Jackie were ecstatic about the new baby. With five years between each of them, and the youngest already seven, all were old enough to avoid jealousy of a new baby.

Like most 17-year-olds, my tall, dark-haired and handsome Johnny spent most of his time away from home. He played football, basketball, and baseball at East High School and had a multitude of good friends. He and his friends were reliable, kind, and caring young men. Johnny had consistently helped me carry the emotional load of our lives, from the day I was in labor with Jessica, when he slipped his little five-year-old hand in mine on the hospital elevator, telling me everything would be okay, up to the acceptance of Kyle as his stepdad. Johnny's huge smile at the news of a fifth child told me all I needed to know about how he felt.

Jessica, at 12, was my smart and beautiful preteen. I tried to make certain her life at 12 didn't resemble mine at the same age by offering encouragement to help her discover her talents. Jessica was an assertive child and a conscientious student who loved athletics, like her brother. She played softball as though the entire weight of each game was hers to bear. She felt a strong sense of duty to her younger siblings.

Our sweet baby, Jackie, at seven, was no longer the baby who almost died from a reaction to a pertussis inoculation at four months of age. Our precious little miracle became her own person and marched to a different drummer early in life. If everyone moved left, she saw the beauty in moving right. Her slightly cock-eyed sense of humor and her parallax view of life delighted and, at times, distressed me, but she always showed me another way to look at most things and broadened my understanding of the world. A new baby in the family was, "Way cool, Mommy!"

Rudy was on duty in Iraq. Kyle had never accepted him into our family. I didn't understand then and I don't understand now. There should always be room in our hearts for another person to love.

On December 8, 2000, James Hall was born; an eight-pound baby at birth, he was comparable with my previous eight-pounders. A good-natured baby with dancing brown eyes, he beguiled all of us with the big, toothless smiles he had for all of his family. Jimmy never wanted for affection from his siblings or his parents.

Kyle's temper in the mornings became worse after Jimmy was born. Another child brought him more stress. One day, when Jimmy was a year old, we had one exceptionally hectic morning. Johnny rode to school early that morning with friends. I was carrying Jimmy down the hall, trying to speed things up with Jessica.

Shane walked out of the bathroom as I went past. I noticed the mess he had left in the bathroom sink and the toothpaste residue running down the cabinet.

"Whoa there, Shane. Looks like you forgot something."

"What?" The look he gave me was a mixture of surprise and obstinacy. He felt privileged, as though the rules of the household didn't apply to him.

"Come on now, stop this. You can clean up after yourself like everyone else in this family."

"Don't you ever talk to my son like that!" Kyle appeared beside me in the small bathroom. He was enraged.

In the mirror, I saw him start to take a swing at me. I dodged the blow and ran, clutching Jimmy to my chest. Kyle chased me upstairs into the laundry room. Fury radiated from him like heat from the sun. I recognized the danger there and was terrified of what might happen. I felt the blow and thought my head would explode from the pain. The next two blows were worse.

My next conscious memory was of an EMT looking in my eyes with a flashlight. There was a cop standing behind him. I could hear the children crying but couldn't see them. Kyle was not in sight.

"My kids, where are my kids?" I was fully conscious. The effort to get off the floor resulted in a massive headache.

"You need to lie still, ma'am. You have a concussion. Your baby and the other kids are fine, but we need to take you to the hospital."

"But they're crying. I need to go to them."

Enormous grief overcame me. I was filled with the immensity of what Kyle's actions meant. I feared my composure wouldn't hold. "No, no hospital. I … I … I have to take my kids to school," I whispered.

The officer leaned over me. "Mrs. Hall, did your husband do this to you?"

I nodded yes through heaving breaths. Our marriage wouldn't survive this day. There was no coming back from what he had done. He had always been able to buy our forgiveness with gifts, but nothing could redeem him now. Our life together was gone in one unveiled fit of anger.

"Your daughter told us your husband is at work?"

"He … he is? He was here when—" I couldn't finish the sentence. Apparently, Kyle had left me unconscious on the floor and gone to work. Jimmy was unharmed when I fell with him in my arms. One of the other kids called 911 for help.

Kyle was arrested at work. A judge issued a restraining order. He wasn't to see James or me for a year. I filed for a separation. He filed for divorce.

Once again, I had allowed myself to marry a man who chose to manage his own stress by striking out at the ones he was supposed to love. Before Kyle's meltdown, we had been in court, trying to save our home from a scam loan operation and an attorney who took our money and gave no services in return. Along with managing a big family, the stress of the court case and a shyster lawyer, Kyle had more than he could handle. He lost control.

Like a lightning strike, the actions of my parents, John, and Kyle coalesced into one thought.

*Isn't it a curious thing that I lived through the same experiences and stresses as all of them and was never tempted to physically beat or denigrate my children or my spouse? There is no excuse powerful enough to explain their behavior. Forgiveness for what they did may not be in me.*

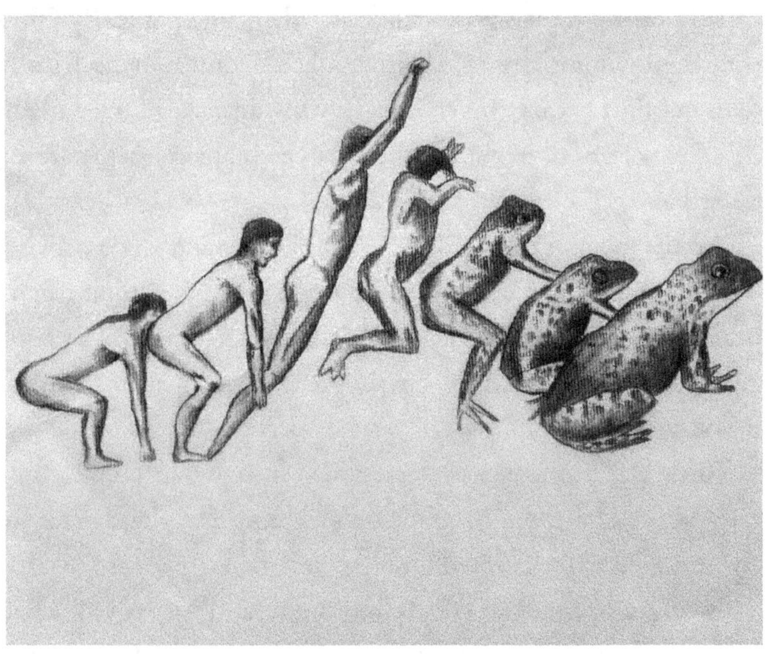

Chapter 20

# Nightmare's End

My nightmare evolved during the 13 years after I researched the cold case files of BTK's victims. In the beginning it was an intense, gut-wrenching horror of a dream, a faceless intruder in my brain dispassionately placing a plastic bag over my face while I watched in frozen terror. After I sketched his face at age 47, the monster became an animated version of my drawings, engendering the same panic. By 2004 the fear in my nightmare was familiar. I didn't make friends with it, but it became much like the constant fear of my parents that I experienced in childhood, a hated staple in my life, unexpected and all consuming.

At the beginning of 2004, my children and I were living happily on our own at a house I bought in the Westlink neighborhood in Wichita. The graphic design business I started allowed me to work from our home and be there for Jessica, Jackie, and Jimmy.

Rudy was in the Marines, stationed in Iraq, with only a military address and the telephone connecting us. The danger he encountered daily haunted us.

Living nearby us in Westlink, Johnny and his wife, Rachel, celebrated their one-year anniversary. They lived in a tiny starter home near St. Francis Church, where they planned their future and the new home they would build together.

A popular junior at Bishop Carroll High School, Jessica played softball and volleyball but enjoyed hanging out with friends most of all. My daughter being out at night terrified me. I was convinced BTK would take her from me.

Jackie, then 10 going on 19, had a passion for softball, like her sister.

Busy being a toddler, Jimmy was my blond-haired, brown-eyed charmer. Everyone in the family spoiled him rotten. My two youngest were with me when they weren't at school. I convinced myself I could protect them from anything if I kept them close, much like I had with my brothers when I was 14 and BTK murdered his first victims.

We struggled financially but found contentment in being together. I continued to jump at shadows and lived every day with a residue of fear that BTK would discover my identity as the person who drew the ever-present pictures of him in the news. I worried that he would find me and hurt my children. I tried concealing my concerns from the kids, but fears like those have residue that is impossible to hide.

"Jessica, wait up. Where are you going?"

"Just over to Kara's to study."

"Come on, Jess, it's almost dark. You know how I feel about you running around after dark."

"Mo-o-om, I'm not running around, Kara lives a half a block from us." Jessica's frustration surfaced. "You want to walk me over there and hold my hand?"

"No, just stay home. You can study together over the phone. No more sarcasm, no more discussion."

"MOM, I'm seventeen years old. It's safe for me to walk half a block in the dark!"

"Don't test my patience, Jessica. I said NO."

She growled something incomprehensible and went to her room, slamming the door behind her.

*Oh, how many times I wanted to do that when I was her age but feared a beating for expressing my anger. I have broken the cycle of abuse with my children.*

It seemed as if I spent half my life worrying about safeguarding my children and the other half listening to them argue with me when I tried to protect them. Their arguments made sense, but I couldn't take the chance of relenting and losing one of them.

January 17, 2004, was the 30th anniversary of the Otero family murders. The identity of their murderer, the BTK serial killer, remained unknown. He destroyed 10 lives and made victims of countless family members, instilling fear in people who lived in the Wichita, Kansas, area between 1974 and 2004.

For 30 years investigators followed hundreds of thousands of leads, publicized a recording of his voice, and analyzed crime scene and DNA evidence. The news media showed my sketches of his face at the age of 47 time and time again. They found nothing substantial enough to identify this waste of human flesh.

Press coverage on the 30th anniversary of the Otero murders was intense in and around Wichita. On January 17, 2004, a writer for the *Wichita Eagle* wrote a story saying he believed BTK was dead.

Television news presented programs that analyzed the past 30 years of the search for BTK. A local attorney, Robert Beattie, published a book, *Nightmare in Wichita*, and newspapers were full of facts, figures, and stories associated with the 10 murders and the man responsible.

Victims' families relived the murders of their loved ones daily through media reports. My sketches of his 47-year-old face, one with a full head of hair, one showing him balding, another clean shaven, and a drawing of him with a mustache were shown extensively in the news. There were no verifiable facts explaining why the BTK killer had not murdered anyone since 1991, but everyone had a theory and voiced it in the media.

On March 19, 2004, the *Wichita Eagle* received a letter with "Bill Thomas Killman" in the return address. It contained a photocopy of Vicki Wegerle's driver's license and photos of her body taken in her bedroom. Police had no photographs of her body at the crime scene; the envelope must have come from her killer. When Vicki's husband found her strangled in their home on September, 16, 1986, he called an ambulance. Before police arrived, she was transported to a local hospital, where she was declared dead. The day the letter was received in 2004, Ken Landwehr, by then Lieutenant Landwehr, was in charge of the investigation. He confirmed that the letter and photographs were from BTK. The photos positively eliminated Vicki's husband as her murderer. For 18 years between 1986 and 2004, Bill Wegerle had lived under the shadow of suspicion for his wife's death. The damage to him and his children during that time could never be undone.

BTK's communications became more frequent in proportion to the intensified media frenzy. The *Wichita Eagle* ran an article on March 24, 2004, titled "BTK Case, Unsolved 30 Years Later" and on April 4, 2004, another article, "Chronicle of a Killer." Both articles detailed the murders and highlighted the investigation.

On May 4, 2004, KAKE-TV in Wichita received a letter containing fake IDs and a word puzzle verified as having come from the serial killer.

On June 9, 2004, at the corner of 1st and Kansas in Wichita, a pedestrian found a package taped to a stop sign. It contained a precise description of the Otero murders.

Ken called me a month later. "Hi, Julie. It's Kenny Landwehr."

"It's good to hear from you. What's going on with the investigation?"

"We're no closer to identifying BTK than we were a year ago, but now he's communicating. Every time the news media runs an article on him, it intensifies his need for attention. He'll make a mistake, and then we'll put him away. A few days ago he dropped off a package at the downtown library. It contained his confession to a murder we know he didn't commit and his threat to murder again. We're getting ready for a news conference and need your drawings."

"Sure, but … uh … I still worry about him coming after me or my kids if my name's linked to the drawings."

"My promise stands. We'll keep your name out of the news. If there is any reference to you at all, it will be as 'The Sketcher.'"

His word was good enough for me. "Thanks, Ken. I can drop them off on my way to work on Monday. Good luck."

The air in the parking garage at City Hall bordered on cool compared to the heat building outside. I followed my well-worn tracks to the detectives squad and dropped off my drawings with Ken. The room was buzzing with their investigation of the new communications from BTK. Ken was busy preparing for the news conference and had no time to talk. He thanked me and I left.

As I opened the door to the garage at the end of the musty smelling hallway leading from City Hall to the parking garage, the temperature difference hit me in the face. The heat and left-over humidity from the previous night's rain gave weight to the air. Fumes expelled by the cars carrying cops, judges, lawyers, secretaries, and administrators to work added to the heaviness.

The building door slammed behind me, the sound echoing off the concrete walls. To my left, in a darkened area at the end of a line of parking spots, a black Jeep Cherokee sat. Its hood was up and a man stood at the front of the car, not looking at the equipment under the hood but staring at people walking into and leaving City Hall. Our eyes met.

*Sweet Jesus. It's* him, *it's the man in my drawings.*

He had a moustache and was balding, a composite of two of my sketches, but it was him. A sound caught in my throat but didn't make it out of my mouth. I turned and rushed back into the building then turned and watched him through the wired-glass window in the door.

He continued to scrutinize the people coming and going, never looking under the hood of his car.

*Oh God, we looked at each other when I was in the garage.*

My hands shook and my heart made a path to my throat. One guy stopped and said something to him, but after a short exchange of words, the guy walked on.

*Call for help … I have to call for help.*

I used the public phone just inside the door and dialed the detectives squad. I looked again to be certain this wasn't one of my false BTK sightings. It wasn't. He was still there, watching the people walking by.

"This is Julie Riedel, I need to talk to Ken Landwehr immediately. It's an emergency."

"Hold on, I'll find him."

*For God's sake, hurry up!*

"Sorry, he already left for the press conference."

"Listen, this is important. I'm in the City Hall parking garage on level four. There's a guy out here who looks exactly like those drawings of BTK that were on television. He's standing outside a black Jeep and has the hood up like his car's stalled, but he's only looking at the people arriving and leaving City Hall; he isn't looking under the hood. You guys need to send somebody up here quick! Level four."

"I'll see if anyone's available."

"No, you don't understand … this is an emer—"

I heard the slam of a car hood closing. A car started. I hung up and ran back to the door in time to see him drive away. His license tag was caked with mud. I couldn't make out the numbers. Hyperventilating, I waited 15 minutes for someone to come down and take my statement. No one came. I began to doubt what I saw. Fearing ridicule, I didn't go back to the squad room to tell them of my sighting. From that day on, I compulsively watched over my shoulder for BTK.

Each time my sketches were included in media stories, police received dozens of phone calls, but none led to a suspect.

*Am I the only person in Wichita who made the connection between one of the drawings and a live person?*

The news release issued several days after he dropped off the package at the library sent a warning that BTK used fake IDs to enter homes. The list of security cautions in the release included, "Don't open your door to strangers." Police directed the warning specifically to people (re: women) living alone.

In October 2004 a manila envelope was left in a UPS box in Wichita. It contained images of children in bondage and a poem threatening the life of lead investigator, Lt. Ken Landwehr.

In December 2004 a walker in Murdock Park discovered a package. It contained Nancy Jo Fox's driver's license and a doll with its hands and feet bound and a small plastic bag over its head.

In January 2005 BTK left a cereal box in the bed of a pickup truck located in a Home Depot parking lot. The owner of the truck threw the box away, thinking it was trash. It was retrieved by police after a separate message from BTK asked what happened to the cereal box. Home Depot had surveillance cameras in the parking lot. Police were able to watch an indistinct person in a black Jeep Cherokee place the box in the pickup truck.

*It had to be the man I saw in the parking garage.*

During February 2005, KAKE-TV received postcards from BTK, and another cereal box was found outside the city on a rural road. In contained a second doll, bound like the first one.

In some of BTK's communications, he alluded to a memoir he was writing titled *The BTK Story*. He wanted to send parts of his manuscript to Lt. Landwehr. In a letter to Ken, BTK asked whether or not information on a "floppy disk" could be traced to the person who made it. Ken responded with a classified ad in the *Wichita Eagle* saying, "Rex, it will be okay." BTK, in his ignorance, trusted the message and sent a disk to KSAS-TV in Wichita. Investigators found embedded metadata from a deleted document on the disk. The deleted data contained the name Christ Lutheran Church. The last person to modify the document was someone with the first name of Dennis.

Checking the internet for people with the first name of Dennis who were associated with the church, police discovered that the president of the church council was a man named Dennis Rader. They drove by his house and discovered a black Jeep Cherokee parked outside. It matched video of the car driven by the person who dropped off the cereal box message at Home Depot during January 2005 and the Jeep I saw in the parking garage.

Dennis Rader was now the task force's prime suspect, but their evidence was only circumstantial, not enough to convict him of murder. They needed a DNA test, which he could refuse if confronted for permission. They secured a warrant to test a DNA sample from Dennis Rader's daughter, obtained from a medical test taken at the medical clinic at K-State, where she attended college. Rader's daughter's DNA was a familial match to the DNA of the skin found under Vicki Wegerle's fingernails. This was the evidence needed to arrest Dennis Rader.

Dennis Rader, at one time or another a quiet assembly line worker at Coleman Company, a security technician with ADT Security Services, a tenacious Code Compliance Officer in Park City, Kansas, Cub Scout leader, and president of his church council was arrested on February 20, 2005, near his home in Park City, Kansas. He lived only a few houses from Marine Hedge, whom he had murdered on April 27, 1985. Wichita police, in cooperation with the Kansas Bureau of Investigation, the Federal Bureau of Investigation, and the Bureau of Alcohol, Tobacco and Firearms, secured evidence from Rader's car, home, backyard shed, and his church.

After his arrest, Rader also directed police to what he called his "mother lode," a drawer in a locked file cabinet at his Park City City Hall office, where he kept newspaper clippings about the case, copies of all of his communications, photographs and other mementos of his victims, several chapters of the book he was writing, which he called *The BTK Story*, and, from the *American Bar Association Journal*, an article titled "How the Cops Caught BTK."

On the morning of February 21, 2005, a little over 31 years after BTK committed his first murder, Wichita Police Chief Norman Williams announced that Dennis Rader had been arrested for the crimes of BTK. When I heard this on my car radio, I pulled over and stopped. I don't know how long I sat staring straight ahead. I took deep drafts of air into my lungs as though I had been holding my breath for 30 years. The sense of relief overwhelmed me.

During 30 hours of testimony, Dennis Rader confessed in cold, factual detail to unlawfully and with malice aforethought taking 10 lives. He was found guilty by virtue of his confession. During his trial, the surviving relatives of his victims described memories of their loved ones and the black abyss of pain of living without the members of their family that this man had murdered without regret. Their stories were alternately filled with poignancy, sadness, forgiveness, and hatred.

The oldest son of Joseph and Julie Otero, BTK's first two victims, spoke directly to the defendant. Charlie Otero spoke of the precious moments he and his surviving siblings would have experienced with their family. Their love for each other was forged with pain and loss, he told the court. He voiced how the surviving family had strayed far from each other over the years, but he, Danny, and Carmen had found their way back to each other, finding a unity and love to be proud of. In the end Dennis Rader failed in his effort to kill the spirit of the Oteros.

Kevin Bright, the lone survivor of an attack by BTK, and the brother Kathryn Bright, reflected the thoughts and words of nearly every family member present during the trial when he said, "At the end of his (Dennis Rader's) life, I hope he stands before the Lord for his judgment. He will spend eternity in darkness."

Stephanie Wegerle Cline, Vicki Wegerle's daughter, spoke for herself and her brother, Brandon, who, as a one-year-old, had been in the house with his mother when she was murdered. Stephanie stated before the court that, "He (Rader) saw she had a family … a little boy there in the house with her, and he showed her no remorse. I ask you today, Your Honor, to show him no remorse. Don't let him have any comfort."

Jeffrey Davis read a prepared speech to Dennis Rader and the court. His mother was BTK's 10th victim, Delores Davis. "…Today, we will each remember a father, a brother, a wife, a mother, a sister, a daughter, a grandmother … all those we love so deeply and still miss so dearly … While you (Rader) agonize over the reality that your last victims were your own family ... we will incorporate into our lives the characteristics modeled by our loved ones: humility, compassion, honor, integrity, kindness, selflessness and love, traits which you are incapable of comprehending."

On August 18, 2005, Dennis Rader was sentenced to 175 years in prison with no chance of parole. He serves his sentence in the El Dorado State Prison in El Dorado, Kansas, living his life in solitary confinement for his own safety; his fellow convicts despise child killers. With deep conviction, I feel he deserved the death penalty, but that was not an option. Kansas reinstated the death penalty in 1994, three years after BTK killed his last victim.

This monster, who was responsible for so much grief in our city, no longer trolled our streets for victims. His evil would never terrorize us in the future. I didn't look over my shoulder again or experience *The Nightmare*. In a moment of realization, I cried from the powerful sense of freedom. My life became clear. I had suffered through a childhood of physical and emotional abuse and married two men who blamed their weaknesses on everyone but themselves. They covered their own pain with anger toward me or with alcohol to forget it.

# Chapter 21

# Now

The hospital room is cold and a dim light above the head of the bed barely illuminates the area. My youngest son lies in the articulated bed as his heartbeats sound in electronic beeps. I listen to him breathe, shallow inhales and exhales, the deep sleep of the young. He is healthy and will be fine, it's just a couple of bruised ribs from horsing around with his friends. The suspected concussion wasn't a concussion. I discovered that a hospital room and my vibrant, boisterous son Jimmy go together like oil and water. He tried to escape before he was admitted, joking with the nurses and doctors that they could surely use his bed for someone who was really sick.

I sit watching him heal and use the time to analyze the secrets of my past.

There are two certainties in my life: my children and my art. They are my reasons to survive. For my kids, I broke the cycle of mistreatment learned during my childhood. I raised them with encouragement, kindness, and love that they can use to enrich their own children's lives. My motivation was to make certain they never felt the aching residue of a mournful childhood such as the one I spent my life trying to overcome.

Painting and sketching are my two unquestioned accomplishments. It isn't necessary for me to know why I'm a good artist. The fact of it is enough. My art has been the single note of comfort since I was old enough to hold a pencil. It's like an old, dear friend and is my solace in difficult times.

I'm not a person who believes I should grow where I'm planted. I'm restless, always searching for the next adventure. It feels liberating to have the freedom to make my own decisions about what to do next. I added singing to my list and just joined a new band as their lead singer.

As a child, being an outstanding sketcher, a singer, or seeking new horizons was not encouraged; most of the time it was dangerous to suggest them. By the time I was a teenager, my only hope was escape: escape to college and, when that dream was crushed, escape into marriage.

Early in my adult life, I expected the abuse that cascaded down on me from the people I should have been able to love, habits left over from my childhood. I was compelled to make the world better for my first husband, but he didn't recognize or appreciate it. When the years rolled by with no improvement, I gave up trying to help him. Life worked better for the children and me when I focused on building a life for them. I pushed past John's resistance and enrolled in college. The successes I had in school lightened my step and made me stronger, while John continued to drown his misery with alcohol and drugs, destroying our marriage.

I saw opportunity in sketching the aging face of a monster whose image held me in the grip of fear for 13 years. The community's fear became a part of me, manifested in horrible nightmares and fear of strangers. The parallel between the BTK serial killer who murdered 10 people and the abuse of my parents who shattered the spirits of their eight children was too clear to ignore. The good news is I lived to continue raising my children on my own terms.

I thought back to the joys of taking care of my children on my own. It was satisfying and exhausting. Satisfying because

I had the opportunity to offer my kids the consideration and reinforcement I wanted for them. Exhausting because we struggled financially for years. I was weary and allowed my tiredness to blind me when I met a man who promised he would love us, honor us, and take care of us. I married him. He worked and cared for us financially, but he used his generosity to buy our forgiveness when he lost his temper until one day his anger spiked, turned to physical violence, and destroyed our marriage permanently. One of the bigger problems was that I allowed my children and me to be responsible for minimizing his anger. We worked hard to avoid the triggers of his wrath at all cost. In the end I realized I had traded my freedom for financial security.

In my quest for answers, I researched the backgrounds of my parents to find reasons for the vicious spitefulness they directed at my brothers and me. Neither of them talked about their childhoods. I found out from relatives that Mom's father committed suicide when she was eight years old. Another relative told me that Mom felt unloved by her mother, my Grandma Mathews, who was shunned by her family because she was an alcoholic. Mom grew up with her stepmother and attended boarding school. She must have been a lonely little girl. She believed all she was told by family members about her own mother and was denied contact with anyone who might love her. She didn't know her mother at all. I saw the similarity. I didn't know my mother at all. I feared my mom. Her loathing left me feeling like an unwelcome outsider in my childhood home. Her actions were that of an unloved child who, as a woman, subconsciously took out the bitterness of her past on her children.

My dad's parents were my Grandma and Grandpa Riedel. Knowing them, I find it hard to believe they could be responsible for his brutish streak. A relative once told me that his parents made life difficult for him, but I have no confirmation from Dad to support that. As a young man, he joined the Marines and became a pilot. When we were kids he talked incessantly about being a Marine. He believed in the Marine Corps way and treated us all like soldiers. We were not allowed to show emotion in his presence. "Marines don't allow their emotions to control them." I can still hear the seething undertones of warning in his voice when he said it. His beatings would get exponentially worse if we cried out or complained in any way.

At my first wedding, when my mother slapped my face, I had the revelation that my mother was cruel to us so our dad wouldn't take out his anger on her for not disciplining us. There are no facts to back up that assumption, but it felt right to me at the time. The years haven't altered my belief. What I know above all else is that I am no longer that abused child. I have forgiven both parents but will never forget.

Jimmy stirred in the bed, moaning. He opened his eyes and gave me a sleepy grin, mumbling something I couldn't understand. I offered him a sip of ice water, but he was asleep again before I made it to the bed.

"How's our patient?" A nurse walked in just ahead of Kyle and disconnected the medical equipment.

Kyle stood close to the bed. "How's he doing?" Jimmy and his dad are close.

Kyle and I cover our painful past with polite conversation. After all these years, Jimmy is the only thing left of our former lives for discussion. Kyle is a different person from the one I married, no longer angry at the world and everyone in it.

"He's fine. He was laughing and joking around with the nurse and me a couple of hours ago. He gave us a hard time about the food they brought for his lunch ... you know, the mystery meat and such."

Kyle laughed. "Did you talk to the doc this morning?"

"Yep, Jimmy should be able to go home in a couple of hours. He said he's going home with you."

Kyle nodded.

Jimmy had a bedroom at each of our houses and stayed where he wanted with no argument from Kyle or me. He's a well-grounded kid.

Kyle turned to me. "You staying? 'Cause if you are, I'll go on to work and come back when he's released. Text me when he's ready to leave."

"Fine with me. I have some work I can do here. I'll tell him you came by."

He left.

I pulled out my canvas pencil rollup and sketch pad and started drawing. Ten lines into the sketch and I was daydreaming about the past again.

Today, I've overcome so many obstacles. I am a classic overachiever, never satisfied with what I have done, always looking for what I can do to provide for my family. It's easy to forget my accomplishments, awards, and honors. I started a graphic design company, Riedel Studio, Inc., after Kyle and I divorced, finding enormous satisfaction in having my own business. When the needs of my kids outstripped the money I brought in, I supplemented our income by teaching technology classes at St. Margaret Mary School in Wichita and as a part-time radio news anchor and reporter. In 2012 I finished a Master's Degree in Information Technology Website Design and Development. I had an offer to be lead designer for a graphic design firm and worked there until 2017 when USD259 offered me a teaching position. Currently, I hold the position of an Art Teacher at Southeast High School in Wichita, Kansas, where I teach drawing and painting classes. In 2019, my second master's was achieved from Fort Hays State University in Educational Leadership. I believe my talents and passion for art needs to be shared and given back. I was nominated and a finalist for the (DCTA) Distinguished Classroom Teacher Award in the spring of 2021-2022.

Resentment from others still puts me on edge. My first instinct is to run away, but I don't. I make a distinction between what I feel and how I react. I push past it, stand up, and reject anyone's attempt to control me with their issues or anger. Their rage is no longer my problem; their bad behavior belongs to them. After "Julie, you're a talented artist, you can do this," it's my secondary mantra.

The future holds whatever adventure comes around the corner and intrigues me. My next great adventure may be Monday. Who knows? Opportunity is right around the corner.

The End

www.ingramcontent.com/pod-product-compliance
Lightning Source LLC
Chambersburg PA
CBHW060923140726

47996CB00001B/355